HEALTH
— IN YOUR —
HANDS

HEALTH
—— IN YOUR ——
HANDS

*A New Look at Modern Palmistry
and Your Health*

BY RITA ROBINSON

Newcastle Publishing

This book is not intended to diagnose, prescribe, or treat any ailment, nor is it intended in any way as a replacement for medical consultation when needed. The author and publisher of this book do not guarantee the efficacy of any of the methods herein described, and strongly suggest that at the first suspicion of any disease or disorder the reader consult a physician.

Edited by Gina Renée Gross
Cover and interior design by Michele Lanci-Altomare
Interior illustrations by Barbara Cunningham
Cover illustration by Barbara Black

Dr. Benjamin Spock's sculpture of hands, courtesy Denis Lee, University of Michigan's director of medical sculpture, affiliated with the Medical Heritage Gallery.

Petroglyphs, courtesy Dan McCarthy, archaeologist, University of California, Riverside.

ISBN: 0-87877-181-6
A Newcastle Book
First printing, 1993
10 9 8 7 6 5 4 3 2 1
Printed in the United States of America.

For

Barbara Cunningham

for unending encouragement and support

TABLE OF CONTENTS

Acknowledgments

The author would especially like to thank Gina Renée Gross, the book's editor, and Michele Lanci-Altomare, the designer, who worked above and beyond the call of duty to produce a quality book. Many thanks also to hundreds of people who have allowed the author to study their hands throughout the years, both in person and through prints.

INTRODUCTION

Palmistry offers insights into a person's mental and physical health, and combined with recent scientific findings, some of which shadow the ancient art of palmistry, they give past, present, and future clues to a person's health.

But as medical findings have changed so, too, must some of the long-held beliefs embraced by palmists.This book discusses those changes, and takes the student of palmistry on a journey from hand reading's earliest beginnings, to where it finds itself today in light of scientific research. The journey is rich with new understanding, but it is also replete with the gold of palmistry's earlier findings. Together, laced with new medical knowledge, they form the basis of *Health in Your Hands: A New Look at Modern Palmistry and Your Health.*

New understandings of the process of aging, the role genetics plays in health, the promotion of healthy lifestyles, and the advent of taking responsibility for one's own health have changed the face of how individuals conduct their lives. No longer does society sit in wonderment over the causes of good and poor health. The reasons are multitudinous. It's known that some aspects of health can be changed, and some can't, as in the case of genetic predispositions to certain conditions.

Yet, knowledge of those conditions, whether they be temporary, or a part of a person's physical makeup, offers the chance to alter or minimize them. Thus, if a person has a genetic predisposition to hypertension, he or she can take early steps to thwart it as much as is humanly possible.

Although likeness exists between the current scientific studies of the hands and ancient palmistry, there are still wide gaps in some instances. In others, though, a long-held traditional belief has found its place in the more recent study of dermatoglyphics. Too, many of the ancient traditions that are presented haven't been corroborated in scientific findings, but are still presented because they are an integral part of palmistry. It is not the intention of this book to prove or refute either scientific research or traditional practices of palmistry as they relate to health. Rather, they are presented as truthfully and as accurately as possible through interviews with medical researchers, from scientific papers and journals, and from my own twenty-four years of study into the ancient art of palm reading, combined with my experiences as a full-time health and psychology writer.

Many researchers in the field of dermatoglyphics, and other medical practitioners who use such manifestations as color, shape, and texture to help in diagnosis, have also been interviewed and the information used in this book.

They include Cheryl Sorenson-Jamison and Robert J. Meier, both anthropologists at Indiana University in Bloomington; Stanley Coren, researcher at the University of British Columbia, Canada; Eugene Scheimann, M.D., private practitioner in Chicago; Marvin Schuster, M.D., Johns Hopkins School of Medicine, Johns Hopkins University, Baltimore, Maryland; Janet H. Silverstein, M.D., University of Florida College of Medicine; Richard V. Lee, M.D., professor of medicine at State University of New York at Buffalo; and Cathy A. Stevens, M.D., University of Utah Medical Center.

Others were interviewed in the normal course of writing health-related articles for magazines, or shared other information on the hands. They include: Jeffrey Prottas, research professor at the Bigel Institute for Health Policy, The Heller School, Brandeis University; Mary Ann Cooper, M.D., associate professor of emergency medicine at the University of Illinois at Chicago; Thomas Mack, M.D., professor of preventive medicine at the University of Southern California School of Medicine; Boonmee Chunprapaph, associate professor of orthopedics, University of Illinois at Chicago; Denis C. Lee, assistant professor of plastic surgery and University of Michigan's director of medical sculpture; and Michael Merzenich, neuroscientist at the University of California, San Francisco.

Because my profession is that of full-time health and psychology writer, and before that, a newspaper reporter with specialties in health, I don't accept as "truth" everything I read or hear about palmistry, and I question everything, including many alternative medical and metaphysical practices. Nor do I accept everything the "scientific community" has to offer, although I have friends and acquaintances within the established medical community.

I agree with Jeffrey Prottas, research professor at the Bigel Institute for Health Policy, The Heller School, Brandeis University, who says, "We feel that technology has arrived and we must accept all of it. How is it that we believe we can't say no?" Prottas was speaking at a biomedical ethics seminar at the University of Southern California Law Center attended by noted scholars, ethicists, and scientists from across the nation.

Yet, when in doubt between what someone "feels" and what science has to offer, I would rely on science, even though it deals with a great many theories. Substance exists, though, behind those theories. And many scientists have proven to be some of our greatest philosophers and thinkers. Consider Albert Einstein who said, "My religion consists of a humble admiration of the illimitable superior spirit who reveals himself in the slight details we are able to perceive with our frail and feeble minds."

So I'm comfortable accepting the hands as something unique, and even spiritual. Perhaps we read the hands because so much energy comes from them. Our lives are centered around their use in work and play. We touch others and make connections with our hands, and they are always available. When we're ill, our hands lack energy. They may feel cold or excessively hot, and we miss the mild warmth they generate when we're feeling good. Our moods are reflected in hand movements, and when we're down, our hands are listless.

They have given me clues to my health. My palms have turned deep red when I'm under stress. My nails have become brittle when I'm not eating right. The Mount of Venus has become hard and not elastic to the touch when I'm negligent of an inner spirituality and sense of love.

This book, though, is not intended to promote self-treatment, or reliance on a palm reader to diagnose or treat illness. I must agree with Michael Murphy, co-founder of Esalen, and a leader in the human potential movement, when his says in his book, *The Future of the Body*, "When given a choice between penicillin administered by a cold clinician and the kindly empathy of a faith healer, anyone with a strep throat would still be best advised to accept the penicillin."

Once, after publication of an article of mine on the hands and health, I received a letter from a woman in another part of the country wanting to know where she could locate a palm reader to help determine her state of health.

My letter to her stated that if she was feeling poorly, or suspected any sort of illness, her best bet was to find a good, reputable physician. If something you find in the hand disturbs you, I would recommend the same thing.

I

AN ILLUMINATED LOOK AT THE HANDS

By understanding our earliest beginnings, we gain knowledge about our past, present, and future lives today. The seeds of our behavior, likes and dislikes, needs and wants were outlined eons ago in the early shadows of primeval forests and verdant savannas. We touch base with our earliest development when we study the hands, and begin to appreciate more the wonder and beauty of our connection to all living creatures, including the human race.

THE HANDS TOUCH EARLY HUMAN HISTORY

Anthropologists note that once early humans stood on their feet, the hands were freed of locomotor activities which enabled them to develop better hand-eye coordination. This ability led to increased tool use, which, in turn, helped develop the brain. Aristotle called the hand "the organ of organs," and Thomas Aquinas paid tribute to the hands by saying, "He [man] has reason and hands whereby he can make himself arms and clothes, and other necessaries of life, of infinite variety."

Figure 1: Ancient hand print contributed by Dan F. McCarthy, a University of California, Riverside archaeologist

We seldom contemplate the beauty and utility of hands, even though they enhance our lives profoundly. We take them for granted without second thought to how they mold a clay sculpture and at the same time shape our lives. Consider Helen Keller who, as a toddler, lost her sight and hearing. At the age of seven she was considered as primitive as an animal. Yet, by age twenty-five she had published her autobiography, spoke three languages and read two, and was enrolled at Harvard University. How did Helen Keller attain all this? Anne Mansfield Sullivan, her tutor and companion who had once been blind, reached the child through the sense of touch. She taught finger language, which involves holding the hand of those with whom a person communicates and imprinting letters of the alphabet. It is a slow process, but physically handicapped individuals have learned to speak, read, and write, and join the world of music, laughter, and love through the sense of touch. Lacking sight and hearing, the sense of touch is enhanced.

But anyone can intensify his or her sense of touch. Not to the degree, perhaps, of a Helen Keller, but in our everyday lives of work and pleasure. We can stop and think about the soft texture of a well-worked piece of leather. Or we can feel the warmth of a stone picked up on a hike. Touching others may be the highest form of the touching experience. When we caress someone, it not only makes him or her feel good, but we enjoy the sensation ourselves. Our mood can change from such a touch. Is it any wonder, then, that the hands continue to intrigue us?

ANCIENT HAND DEPICTIONS

The importance of the hand's contribution to understanding the human psyche and body is prehistorical. An aboriginal Indian petroglyph found in Nova Scotia depicts a hand showing the flexion creases, including the lines of Life, Head, and Heart in palmistry, and dermal ridge fingerprints and mount patterns. Palm and fingerprint patterns have also been found at early American Indian sites, and elsewhere throughout the world at ancient site excavations.

After viewing cave paintings from several ancient sites, Jacob Bronowski, twentieth century mathematician, statistician, inventor, and historian, writes in *The Ascent of Man* that "there are many gifts that are unique in man; but at the centre of them all, the root from which all knowledge grows, lies the ability to draw conclusions from what we see to what we do not see, to move our minds through space and time, and to recognize ourselves in the past on the steps to the present. All over these caves the print of the hand says: `This is my mark. This is man.'"

The accompanying photo (figure 1), contributed by Dan McCarthy, a University of California, Riverside archaeologist, shows ancient hand signatures found in southern California. Called "petroglyphs," they are carvings in rock made by using a hammer and chisel. "The markings that form the hand are very precise, and the hand of the person doing the work probably was used as the model," says McCarthy. "Petroglyphs and pictographs of ancient humans are a fairly universal sign of individuality—a signature. It might be similar to the way we discuss fingerprinting, although the hand signatures have a deeper meaning. Many times ancient humans painted their hands (pictograph) and used them as a stamp or imprint."

Fingerprint designs found on the walls of a neolithic burial passage on an island near Brittany are thought by some to represent an early understanding of dermatoglyphics, which is the current name for the

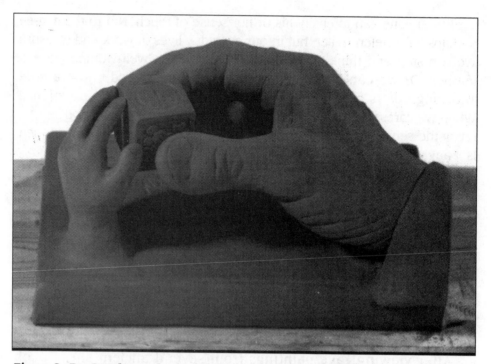

Figure 2: Dr. Spock's sculptured hand cast in preparation for bronzing, courtesy of Dr. Denis Lee & the Medical Heritage Gallery, Waco, Texas

scientific medical studies of palm and fingertip ridge formations (see Chapter 6). Other scientists, though, point out that the prehistoric representations of ridge patterns could simply be designs taken from nature, which are similar to the arches, whorls, and loops found on the fingers and mounts of the hands. Whatever the reason for the designs, it is clear that men and women have always been intrigued by hands.

IMMORTALIZED HANDS

The medical community is no exception when it comes to finding fascination in the hands. Reproductions of the hands of some of the world's most famous living physicians have been immortalized in bronze by University of Michigan's director of medical sculpture, Denis C. Lee, who recalls that famous pediatrician Dr. Benjamin Spock has "big hands with spatulated fingertips," a term long used in palmistry to describe a highly creative individual. See accompanying photo (figure 2) of Spock's sculptured hand cast in preparation for bronzing.

World-famous heart surgeon Michael E. DeBakey, M.D., and pediatrician Benjamin Spock, M.D., are but a few of the medical greats whose healing hands Lee, who is also a professor of art and assistant professor of plastic surgery, intends to sculpture. To capture the essence of DeBakey's hands, Lee observed the noted heart surgeon's hands before, during, and after surgery, and at sittings. He noted the exceptionally long, thin fingers. "They were nearly like someone with acromegalia, or like Abe Lincoln, who had the disease; they were extremely long and dexterous. Most surgeons have small hands."

Lee remarked to DeBakey that his hands looked like the typical hands of musical geniuses. He said Debakey responded, "If I had not been a surgeon, I would have been a musician." Due to the extreme length of his fingers, Debakey wore custom-designed surgical gloves made from a mold of his hands. Lee echoes the sentiments of many people who are intrigued by hands when he says, "There is something about hands that I think is just fascinating. They're as important to your character as your face."

Many scholars and adherents of palmistry attribute hand reading as we know it today to the ancients of India. Some, though, say modern palmistry stemmed from Ancient Greece through the Greek pantheon of Gods. And still others say the Greeks and Romans borrowed it from the Egyptians. Some forms of hand reading, though, existed before written history, and are found in prehistorical cave art, which only shows that men and women have found the hands intriguing since the beginning of time, and it was included in the schooling of ancient prophets and diviners in many civilizations.

THE HAND AND BRAIN CONNECTION

Contemporary scientists know that direct links to the brain exist in the hand. Studies on monkeys at the University of California, San Francisco show that when a finger is tapped at set intervals for an extended period of time, the map of the brain changes. The basic nerve cell (neuronal) connections in the region affected grew in response to the increased input from the finger. At the same time, the neuronal connections in another area of the brain not being used decreased.

Neuroscientist Michael Merzenich, who conducted the studies, said that to understand the process of what's happening with the monkey, we need to understand the neuronal grouping and growth in humans beginning with the developing fetus. As the brain grows, nerve cells sprout thousands of projections, called axons, in the motor area of the brain that generate movement of the fingers. Brain representations of skin surfaces of the hands are constantly changing as we change what we do with our hands.

"The studies we're doing involve representations of the hand-brain itself. We know that if you consider representation of the hands and brain, it is alterable. If you have a predominant use, and it delivers input into the brain in a temporal form, that portion of the brain will change. As a skill improves, involving greater brain use, the temporal form changes. On the simplest level, if a person is in an occupation with defined finger use, it creates changes in the brain that are reconstructible and really are the basis of those proven skills," says Merzenich.

"If I use my hands in some new refined or high level way, and also make adjustments in the more complex uses of my hand, then the representation in the brain is further changed. For example: the haptic ability [science of the sense of touch] to identify three dimensional objects by hand recognition is one of the highest levels of hand operation," he says. Merzenich mentions Helen Keller as a prime example of how the sense of touch can foster the highest levels of hand/brain operation.

Those same studies show that loss of a finger totally changes the map of the brain normally responding to that finger. Also, the research at UCSF isn't entirely new. C. Wolff, an endocrinologist, said in the 1940s that the hand and a certain part of the cortex of the brain retained imprints of muscular patterns formed by countless habitual repetitions of movements. Although the brain-finger research claims no connection to palmistry, it does indicate that swimming around in the soup of scientific research are anomalies that may clear the air as to why some of the long-held beliefs of this ancient practice have some scientific validity.

Other research, too, adds to the brain-hand connection. Experiments by computer scientist Thea Iberall at the University of Southern California suggest that the hand is controlled by "virtual fingers" in the brain—cerebral instructions to your hands that don't necessarily correspond to actual fingers. The idea behind the conceptual model, called virtual fingers, is that hand movement depends more on how the brain perceives specific hand function, than on how the brain conceives the specifics of hand anatomy.

For instance: Iberall says the brain instructs a person to use two virtual fingers, meaning two opposing forces, to pick up an item. The thumb, serving as a one-finger force, works in conjunction with the other four fingers acting as one force. In other words, these four fingers act as if they were one finger, or a virtual finger, to gather sensory information for the brain. The study's initial purpose is to develop improved prosthetics for those with missing hands.

THE MIND/BODY CONNECTION

Although our genes carry the blueprints of certain health conditions, we are free to a certain degree to guide and control them through our thoughts and actions. Thus, if the hands indicate an inherited tendency to heart problems, the individual, rather than discounting the finding or assuming that nothing can be done, can make certain his or her lifestyle is conducive to protecting the heart. Healthful diets and exercise become important, but so does the realization that a healthy mind, capable of coping with stress (since stress will never be eliminated from life), dealing with anger in a positive manner, and developing some form of spirituality, serve as bulwarks against poor health. Personality and temperament as shown in the hands will be discussed throughout this book since the mind/body/spirit of an individual is markedly linked to health.

Hand reading, though, is not new to the world of medicine. In the Middle Ages, palmistry was included in the curriculum of medical schools. One of the first books printed on the Gutenberg printing press in 1475 was one written by Aristotle on palmistry, and the father of modern medicine, Hippocrates, is said to have discovered a correlation between the hand and the condition of the lungs.

Although a majority of traditional physicians in the twentieth century have routinely scoffed at palm reading, scientific studies at leading research universities in the past few years indicate that some signs of impending illnesses, genetic abnormalities, and psychological problems may appear in the hands long before more noticeable signs become evident. The new studies, some under the heading "dermatoglyphics," go beyond the frontiers of palmistry, yet bear some resemblance to that ancient art, and in some cases, mimic it.

OLD PREJUDICES AND NEW FINDINGS

Dermatoglyphic scientists today are interested in defining the process that underlies the formation of particular ridge patterns on the palms and feet (see Chapter 6). What, indeed, causes specific patterns to emerge? The technology available makes such studies more scientific, since many of the earlier ones were done by observation. Still, many of the early theories about a brain-hand connection have proven correct.

Too, many other earlier hand observations, not necessarily entailing dermatoglyphics, have proven false. For example, in the early 1900s, some medical practitioners who observed the hands believed that certain line formations on the palm were an indication of homosexuality. The assumption has proven to be incorrect, but reflects biases of the medical establishment at that time who thought homosexuality was a mental disease, or at the least, abnormal. I've studied the hands of many gay and lesbian people and never found a particular marking that sets them off as any different than their heterosexual counterparts. Like anyone else, gays and lesbians are capable of being loving, cold, temperamental, kind, mean . . . and showing any other emotion or personality trait available to humankind.

Other biases have also existed through the years. It was once believed that a stiff, low-set thumb, combined with short fingers, belonged to a "more primitive" type individual. Wrong again. Findings like those and others, some of which are still in use today, reflect the prejudices and biases of the time. For example, the accompanying print (figure 3) showing short fingers in comparison to the rest of the hand belongs to an author of several horror fiction books. He also possesses a master's degree in psychology and has an IQ exceeding 145.

MORE BRAIN POWER

Another contributing factor to the shapes of the hand is linked to the way a person holds them. Many palmists have long believed in a direct

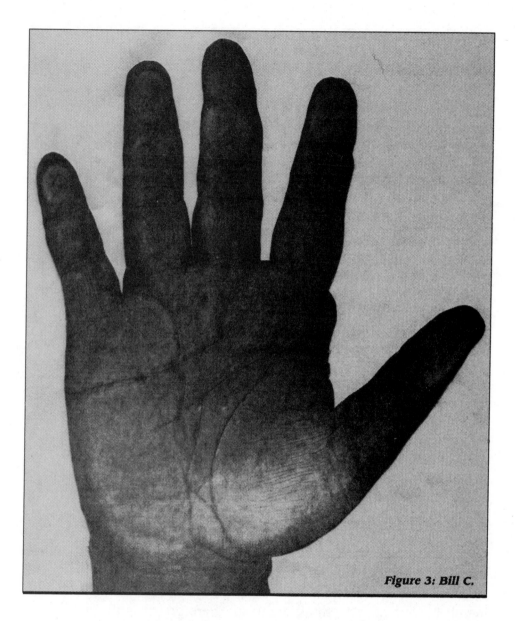

Figure 3: Bill C.

link between the brain and such manifestations as thumb arch, space between fingers, and even the length of fingers in comparison to one another, since this comparative link can be determined by the way we hold our hands. For example, if a ring finger normally appears to be longer than the index finger when the hand is held flat, we can, by concentrating, force the index finger to appear longer by straining the

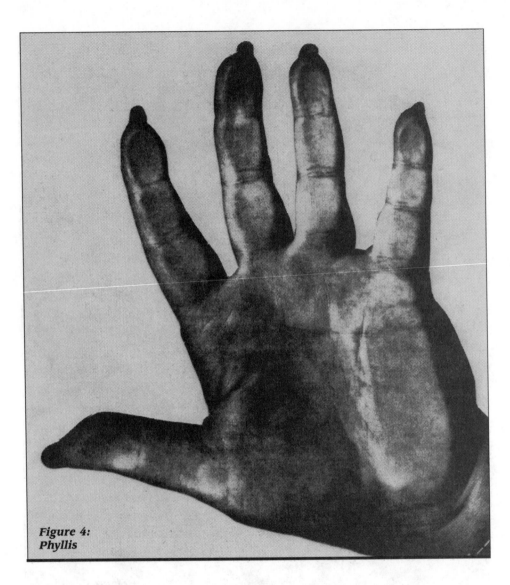

Figure 4:
Phyllis

hand. But we have to think about it. Therefore, it is the normal, or relaxed, position of the fingers that tells us something about the individual's personality. Since portions of the brain develop in accordance with the use and carriage of the hands, then we can outwardly witness the makeup of an individual.

The accompanying prints (figures 4 and 5) show how a person can alter the alignment of fingers when he or she makes a concerted effort to do so. Figure 4 shows the ring finger longer than the index

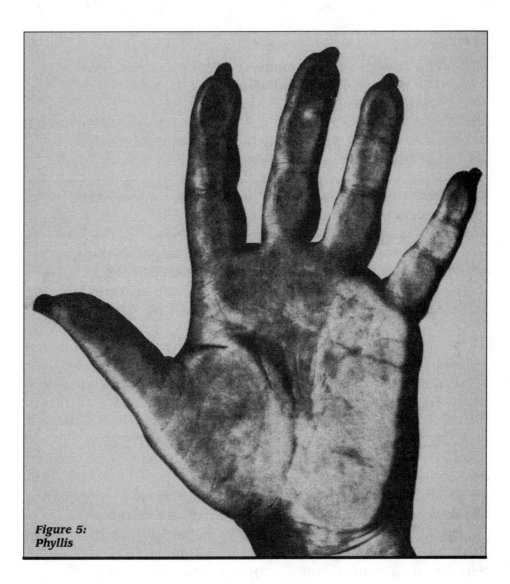

Figure 5:
Phyllis

finger, and was accomplished by forcing the fingers into an unnatural alignment. Figure 5 of the same hand shows it in its natural position.

Thus the brain is always engaged consciously and unconsciously during hand movement, just as it is for facial expressions. We can try to conceal an emotion, such as holding a straight face when we really want to laugh, but a careful observer will note a slight twitch or other facial motion.

The *Bible* contains many references to the hand. The following are taken from *The New Oxford Annotated Bible*:

☞Proverbs, 3:16—Long life is in her right hand; in her left hand are riches and honor.

☞I Samuel, 26:18—For what have I done? What guilt is on my hands?

☞Revelation, 14:9—And another angel, a third, followed them, saying with a loud voice, "If any one worships the beast and its image, and receives a mark on his forehead or on his hand, he also shall drink the wine of God's wrath. . .

☞Proverbs, 24:33—A little sleep, a little slumber, a little folding of the hands to rest, and poverty will come upon you like a robber. . .

Some Chinese scholars consider palmistry as an offshoot of physiognomy, which is the study of facial expressions and features.

Through careful observation of the hands, a palmist, too, can detect the inner signs portrayed by the conformation of the hand. It becomes important, therefore, for the palm reader to establish a relaxed atmosphere in which to read someone's hands since the subject will be more likely to relax his or her hands into their natural position.

We have traced the hands from their earliest beginnings, through ancient observations, to modern day studies. What seems most striking is that they have always intrigued humans, and will continue to do so in new and innovative ways. Understanding them can lead to knowledge about the health of our minds, bodies, and spirits, which are, in effect, our whole selves.

Humans and other primates share the following hand traits:

☞They have nails instead of claws on their hands and feet.

☞They have prehensile (adapted to grasping) hands and feet.

☞They are equipped with five fingers and five toes on each hand and foot.

☞Thumb and toe are opposable to the remaining digits.

☞Print patterns on the hands and soles of feet are apparent.

II

DIFFERENCES IN THE RIGHT AND LEFT HANDS

Determining whether a person is predominantly right- or left-handed is important in reading the hand, since certain characteristics normally associated with right/left brain thinking are shifted. Also, since the nondominant hand contains information about the person's childhood predispositions, it must be studied in order to understand the changes that have occurred to make the person who he or she is today.

WHICH HAND IS DOMINANT?

Acquiring the predominant use of the right hand took millions of years, and may have begun when humans commenced to hunt and forage for food, making it necessary to develop specialized use of one or the other hand. As the preference for one hand for certain tasks evolved, the hemispheres of the brain also developed accordingly into specialized areas. Some anthropologists believe that when humans began talking it caused the predominant use of the right hand since speech is associated with the left hemisphere of the brain, which controls activity on the right side of the body. When a person is left-handed, the usual activities associated with the right or left hemispheres of the brain are frequently altered.

Medical researchers have established certain criteria for determining if a person is left- or right-handed. In one large study, people tested were considered right-handed if they used the right hand for writing, throwing, sewing, hammering, sawing, shooting marbles, bowling, knife use, or scissor or spoon use. If they used the left hand for any of these functions, they were considered left-handed.

Most palm readers ask a person which hand he or she uses the most. If the person claims to be ambidextrous, it usually means he or she is predominantly right-handed, but uses the left hand for certain functions. As the reading progresses, it may become apparent from other markings that the person is more left-handed. Only by thoroughly studying both hands can this be determined.

It is important to establish which hand is dominant because the less dominant hand signifies hereditary temperament, skills, potential, and likes and dislikes. It reveals early childhood influences. The dominant hand also shows these characteristics, but demonstrates what the person has made of his or her inherited tendencies and family influences.

When the two hands are compared, the markings on one are usually slightly different than the other. Occasionally, a vast difference exists, and this gives the reader vital clues about how the early life and inherited tendencies have been used. When reading palms, the right hand (on a right-handed person) is considered the dominant hand. It is the hand of the present and the future. The opposite is true of the left-handed person; the left hand is considered dominant and tells of the present and the future.

DIFFERENCES IN READING THE PALMS

Since the nondominant hand displays the person's background, major differences give clues as to what the person has done with inborn traits. If the lines of the right hand (visa versa on the left-handed individuals) are more robust, deep, long, or travel to different locations than what is shown on the opposite hand, the individual has used his or her innate abilities to his or her own betterment. If the lines, though, are not as pronounced on the dominant hand, it is well to study them and see if the person has not yet reached his or her potential or is frittering away talents and abilities.

Conversely, if the lines are stronger on the dominant hand, he or she may have overcome great obstacles. A good example of this is the Line of Life found circling the Mount of Venus on the thumb side of the palm. It may be weaker on the nondominant hand, and much stronger on the dominant hand. This indicates people who have made good use of their innate abilities and, perhaps, grown beyond the confines of their childhoods.

Often, when individuals evolve from troubled childhoods, but have put the past behind them and gone on to achieve more than they ever expected, the dominant hand will far surpass the strengths found in the nondominant hand. Yet, traces of the childhood may still be found in markings on the dominant hand.

Many people who excel in their chosen fields have come from troubled childhoods. One psychologist I know claims that such people "have been tested in the fire," and use the strengths they gained to propel them forward. The same is true of poor health in childhood— even disabilities. Some are able to grow despite handicaps. A childhood of struggle has given them the strengths they need for achievement in other areas of their lives.

A recent newspaper article suggests that dieters who are right-handed should switch to the left hand when eating as it slows down consumption. In so doing, a person is also altering the use of his or her brain by switching to the more creative side.

INHERITED HEALTH CHARACTERISTICS

Health conditions that might be inherited may first display themselves in the nondominant hand. Therefore, if the nondominant hand shows a propensity toward heart trouble, and the marking is also found in the dominant hand, the person can be warned to take extra precautions concerning the inborn trait. It doesn't necessarily mean the person is going to suffer the consequences of his or her hereditary trait, but if the person is aware of it, he or she can take precautions to lessen its effects.

Perhaps the nondominant hand indicates an inborn worrying temperament, such as a network of fine, tiny lines covering the palm. If the dominant hand also shows this trait, it indicates the person likely will continue to be a worrier, which can be detrimental to health. If the dominant hand, though, is clear of this trait, it indicates the person has knowingly taken steps to overcome his or her worrying nature. Those still bearing this fine network of lines on both hands can also be encouraged to develop life patterns than will lessen their inborn worrying nature. Fine markings such as worry lines do diminish when efforts are made to change behavior.

Several notables throughout history have been identified as being left-handed. They include three American presidents: Gerald Ford, Ronald Reagan, and George Bush. Ben Franklin was left-handed; so were Albert Einstein, Alexander the Great, Joan of Arc, and Queen Victoria. Artists Leonardo da Vinci, Raphael, Pablo Picasso, and Michelangelo serve as testimony to the talents of left-handers. Other notables include Paul McCartney, Babe Ruth, Whoopie Goldberg, and Harpo Marx.

THE INNER LIFE OF THE INDIVIDUAL

Some palmists believe the nondominant hand denotes the inner life of individuals. Characteristics they try to cover up, or gloss over, such as an inability to say what's really on their minds, may show up in the nondominant hand, but not the dominant hand. Thus, even though a person may appear to have an assertive nature, he or she may back off when the chips are down. The true nature shown in the nondominant hand comes forth. For example, the thumb and Finger of Saturn (the middle finger) may show themselves relaxed and supple on the right hand, indicating an open-minded, noncritical person. But on the nondominant or left hand, these same fingers may be stiff, indicating that the person may be hiding qualities he or she doesn't desire in the face shown the world.

Another example might be seen in the Finger of Mercury (little finger). It may appear long and straight on the dominant hand, indicating a person who is a natural public speaker. Yet, on the nondominant hand, it might appear shorter and slightly bent. By comparing the two hands, the reader can determine if the individual is really a shy person who has worked hard to overcome the trait. Or, it can indicate someone who is overtly shy, but who really wishes to be more open and communicative.

When studying hands, it is important to make people feel comfortable with these findings, and show other strengths they may have, or that will help them either overcome their shyness, or to realize that shyness can sometimes be an asset. Although Americans don't value shyness like some other cultures, including some of this country's Native Americans, Asiatics, and Hispanic populations, shy people are often more sensitive to others than the norm. Also, being shy doesn't mean not being assertive. Some shy people just go about getting their way in a different manner—often very effectively.

LEFT-HANDEDNESS

It would seem that with 10 to 15 percent of the American population (twice as many men as women) being left-handed, it would be more accepted in society to have a dominant left hand. Yet, the left hand is continually maligned. For example, we talk about a "left-handed compliment." Too, a "left-handed handshake" is considered bad manners, a "left-handed devil" is shown on ancient tarot cards, and a "left-handed oath" isn't considered binding.

Until recently, and sometimes still, left-handed children were encouraged to use their right hands, often with harsh measures. Trying to force a change results in confusion since handedness involves specific development in the right and left hemispheres of the brain. The right hemisphere of the brain is more developed on left-handed individuals. The left hemisphere is the more dominant on a right-handed person. This, however, does not preclude a right-handed individual from being talented since it is a popular notion that

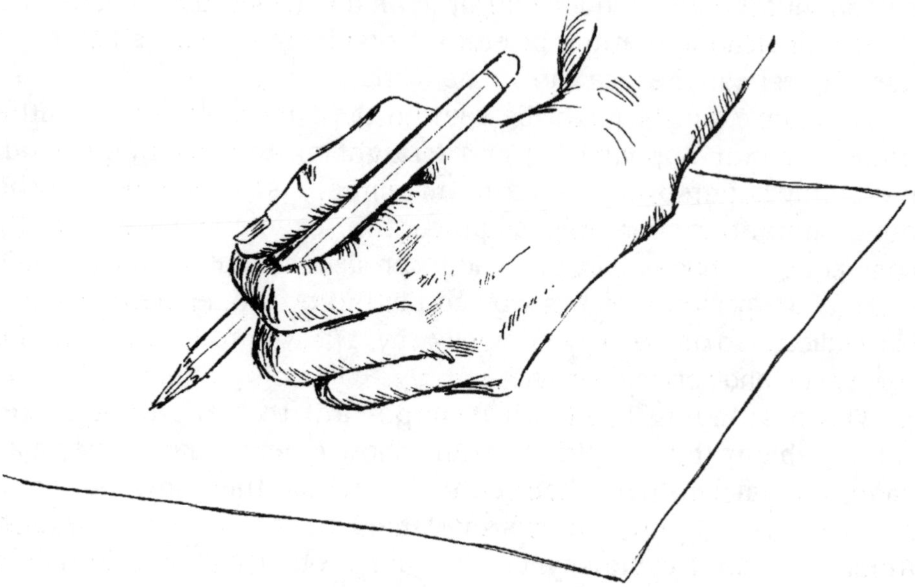

Figure 6: Drawing of someone using his or her left hand

creativity lies on the right side of the brain. In actuality, there is far more involved in creativity as far as the brain goes than predominance of a certain hemisphere.

Researcher Stanley Coren of the University of British Columbia in Vancouver, who identifies left-handedness through dermatoglyphics (the study of skin ridge patterns on the hands and feet that is discussed in Chapter 6), and who developed the classification of eight fingerprint prototypes, says, "We recently collected data from nearly 2,200 individuals on whether or not they are left- or right-handed. We found that the patterns between left- and right-handers is, in fact, different. What you find is that the left-handers have simpler patterns. They tend to have more arch patterns and fewer whorls. And we found that the biggest difference between the left- and right-handers is in the ring finger."

Left-handed people also tend to have radial loops, which are found on only about 2 percent of the population, according to Coren. A radial loop, which comprises the center of the fingerprint, is like an inverted

"U" that tilts toward the little finger. Right-handers can also have these formations, but the chance of being left-handed is doubled if there are radial loops.

His studies also show that identical twins have the same fingerprint patterns, which he says isn't surprising since, prior to the advent of blood testing, fingerprints were used to determine if twins were identical or fraternal. Recent studies of identical twins at the University of British Columbia in Vancouver, Canada, though, show that identical twins do not share exactly the same genetic makeup. The difference is small, perhaps only 5 percent, but it can account for vast differences—such as one twin having an abnormality such as Down's syndrome and the other not.

What Causes Left-Handedness?

A greater proportion of left-handed than right-handed people tend to suffer from dyslexia, learning disabilities, schizophrenia, autism, and other genetically based abnormalities, which have been traced to abnormal hormonal fluctuations, or environmental stresses (such as exposure to chemicals) in the womb before the fourteenth week of gestation.

The emotional state of the mother can also cause these hormonal fluctuations. According to Linda Lee and James Charlton, authors of *The Hand Book*, a study reported in the *New York Times* in 1959 indicated that the number of left-handers increased during times of war and a depressed economy. It's hypothesized that sometimes stress on the mother affects fetal development of the nervous system, which occurs at the same time formation of the skin's dermal ridges takes place. This occurs prior to the fourteenth week of gestation, and involves the flow of testosterone on the developing fetus. Thus, a map of this development is laid down in the hand.

Left-handedness may not be entirely due to genetic differences, however. The condition can be caused by stress at birth, such as prolonged labor, says Coren. Studies also indicate that oxygen deficiency associated with birth, and which causes complications, affects the brain's left hemisphere by neutralizing the inborn right-sided tendency. Left-handedness is more common among infants who need resuscitation at birth. Multiple birth also appears to increase the tendency toward left-handedness, and if both complications are present—multiple birth, plus the need for resuscitation—the risk of left-handedness is further increased.

Further research, however, raises the possibility that the conditions that lead to some types of birth complications were established in the fetus before the onset of labor. Thus, left-handedness can be (1) genetic, (2) manifested in the womb, or (3) caused by stress at birth. In the first instance of a genetic predisposition, the outcome is dictated by heredity, and is the natural tendency of the individual. In the latter two instances concerning fetal or birth complications, the left-handedness is considered a pathologic shift, and is not the natural tendency of the individual, although he or she will go through life as a left-hander.

Lois Ruby of Minneapolis runs a mail-order business catering to items designed for left-handers. For a catalog of items, send $2.00 to 210 W. Grant, Unit 215, H.H., Minneapolis, MN 55403. For information about *Left Hander Magazine*, published by Left Handers International, write Box 8249, Topeka, KS 66608. Subscription is fifteen dollars per year.

The Effects of Left-Handedness

"Left-handed people get the short end of the stick," says Coren. "Statistically they have reduced life spans and other problems such as allergies, sleep difficulties, and slower maturation. Too, the stress of living in a right-handed world may reduce their survival rate." A good portion of studies on survival rates of left-handers involved the use of statistics on baseball players, since the material included whether or not they were left-handed. Life spans were evaluated, and the left-handed baseball players appeared to have shorter life spans. Other studies, too, in the general population, indicate shortened lives for lefties.

The stress of living in a right-handed world, with everything from door knobs to safety switches on power equipment being on the right hand, is evident. Another of Coren's studies showed that left-handers are more likely than right-handers to have accidents that require medical attention. Other studies indicate that, proportionality, left-handers have greater frequencies of depression and attempted suicides. Also, over half the babies born with extremely low birth weight are left-handed, and women over forty have a doubled chance of giving birth to a left-handed child. Too, if both parents are left-handed, they have a four times greater chance of having a left-handed child than if neither parent were left-handed, thus building a case for genetic influence.

Although disagreement exists on whether left-handedness is genetic or the result of prenatal injury, it is known that neurologically the left hemisphere of the brain (which is dominant in right-handed people) is more vulnerable to prenatal injury than the right hemisphere. So it's postulated that prenatal injury affects the left side, causing birth complications, resulting in a dominance shift leading to left-handedness.

Studies at Washington University School of Medicine, St. Louis, propose that antipsychotic drugs which help reduce some of the more bizarre symptoms of schizophrenia, work by regulating interactions between the left and right hemispheres of the brain. Other studies on the link between left-handedness and learning disabilities are being conducted at The New York Hospital-Cornell Medical Center. Doctors there believe that the male hormone, testosterone, may be responsible for some learning disabilities. Previous studies show that males have more learning disabilities. Prenatal exposure to the male hormone appears to account for the excess of left-handers among males, suggesting that handedness is biologically determined before it is expressed. Not all lefties, of course, have learning disabilities, schizophrenia, or other handicaps.

On the positive side, some research indicates that 40 percent of left-handers use both sides of the brain to process speech, whereas right-handers process it almost solely it in the left hemisphere. This ability allows some left-handers to recover more readily from strokes, which more readily affect the left side.

From the studies, the indication is clear that something is going on in the brain that affects hand use, and is not to be overlooked in the study of the hands and health. Nor to be overlooked is the fact that more attention is being given to left-handers than ever before.

No longer are most subjected to the torture of a forced change in hand use. A majority of parents and educators recognize that forcing a change isn't healthy, and only results in a frustrated left-handed person. No amount of force will change the wiring in the brain. So it's up to the right-handed public to change its attitude about its left-handed brothers and sisters, rather than for the lefties to try to become right-handed.

The palm reader must also be sensitive to the handedness of the person whose hand he or she is reading. Once hand dominance has been established, a more accurate reading becomes possible. Although the dominant hand remains the major source of the person's past, present, and future lives, the nondominant hand provides background information that is important for a thorough understanding of what helped shape the person to begin with. When questions or doubts arise while reading the dominant hand, one can always compare it to the nondominant hand for additional clues.

III

TEXTURE, COLOR, AND TOUCH IMPRESSIONS

Most palmists take note of the texture, color, and temperature of the hand before beginning a reading. It gives them important information about the person's temperament and personality, and also how he or she is feeling at the moment.

TEMPERATURE

Room and outside temperature must be taken into consideration when color and feel of the hand are evaluated. Temperature of the hands, like color, can be changeable, so some signs indicated apply only for chronic conditions. Accordingly, the hands are usually pinker in a warm room, and pale to white in a cold setting. The person's mood and nervous system, as well as room temperature, can influence the color and temperature of the hand. Also at work is a person's autonomic nervous system, of which he or she has little control.

☞ ─────────────────────────────────────

> An ancient tradition regarding hand temperature borrows from astrology:
>
> ☞ **Hot and wet is the earth sign, and signifies moodiness.**
>
> ☞ **Cold and dry is an air sign, and means cheerfulness.**
>
> ☞ **The fire sign is hot and dry, and designates a volatile type personality.**
>
> ☞ **A cold and wet hand is under the water sign, and stands for lack of emotion.**

AUTONOMIC NERVOUS SYSTEM

Many observable conditions are tied to our sympathetic and parasympathetic nervous systems, which are a part of the overall autonomic nervous system that controls and regulates the parts of the body which we don't consciously regulate. This includes the heart, some muscles, and the glands.

In recent years it has been found that we can gain some control over the autonomic nervous system through biofeedback and meditation, particularly helpful in controlling stress. These systems are in control when a person blushes because it widens small blood vessels in the face due to an emotional response. It happens automatically without the person's control.

The sympathetic nervous system, one of two parts to the autonomic nervous system, accelerates the heart rate, raises blood pressure, and narrows blood vessels. In effect, it "warms us up." The parasympathetic nervous system, does the opposite. It slows the heart rate, increases gland activity, and relaxes some muscles. It can make our bodies cold, our faces turn pale.

Dr. Charlotte Wolff writes in *A Psychology of Gesture*, that when we're depressed the parasympathetic system "goes into action and makes itself felt by an oppressive feeling in the region of the heart and in a general state of displeasure and tension, in paleness of the face, as well as by cold hands and feet. . . ." Palm readers surmise that cold hands can indicate tension, unhappiness, grief, self-doubt, or a fearful nature. When we feel happy, and full of self-esteem, our blood freely circulates, causing our hands and feet to warm.

COLOR OF THE PALMS

The color of the skin on the hands is first determined by the amount of melanin in the basal (bottom) portion of the epidermis and is hereditary. The psychological and physical aspects of the palm's color, according to classical palmistry, have the following meanings:

○ A generally pale color shows a lack of energy and concern with oneself, rather than those around him or her.
○ White or pale palms show lack of warmth and a "cool" attitude toward life. White palms can also indicate insufficient blood flow, lack of vitality, anxiety, or illness.
○ Yellow-tinged palms can indicate exposure to toxins, or chemicals in the system (such as additives) that a person can't tolerate. Some people, however, aren't bothered by additives. Yellow-tinged hands can also indicate pessimism, caution, a worrying nature, and an uneven temper.
○ Pink palms generally belong to a well-adjusted, outgoing individual, with lasting energy.
○ Red palms belong to people who are full of energy, coupled with enthusiasm, optimism, and the ability for deep concentration. They can be overly assertive or aggressive at times. Materialism is shown by extreme red hands.
○ Deep red or purplish palms belong to moody people, who move slowly, and often think slowly.
○ Blue-tinged palms are found on people with circulatory problems. They often lack energy.

The colors, as interpreted by classical palmistry, predate some of the findings used by medical practitioners today. Interpreting hand color can be one of the first steps on the trail to uncovering important information regarding a person's state of health, whether it be involved with the physical working of the body or with the temperament of the individual.

MEDICAL INTERPRETATIONS OF COLOR

According to Richard V. Lee, M.D., professor of medicine at State University of New York at Buffalo, alcoholism and cirrhosis of the liver produce red-looking palms caused by vascular dilation. A blue tint to the hands is indicative of poor circulation or problems with the lungs; a yellow color might be seen on someone who is jaundiced, who smokes, or who works with certain toxic chemicals. People with particularly high blood fat levels may also have a yellowish tinge to the hands.

Lee cautions that pregnant women also develop palmar erythema, a redness in the thenar (Venus) and hypothenar (Luna) areas of the hands, related to hormones during pregnancy. "If you see a really red hand on a pregnant woman you worry about that," he says.

THE SKIN OF THE HAND

Skin is the largest organ of the body. The three main layers of skin include the outer or protective layer called the "epidermis." Next is the "dermis," or middle layer, containing connective tissue composed of blood vessels and nerves. The "subcutis," or bottom layer, is made up of fatty tissue to help protect the muscles and bones.

A hand wound is "healed" when new cells mature and move up through the layers of cells to the outer layer, taking different forms through the layers until they reach the top. The outer layer consists of scaly plaques of dead cells, and is thickest in the body areas subject to the most use, such as the palms of the hands.

Skin Texture

Skin texture refers to the thickness of a person's skin on the palms, which involves the depth and breadth of the skin ridges. It can range from very thin, with seemingly very little protrusion from the ridges, to very thick, whereby the ridges are easily identified. Finer skin patterns are usually found on conic and philosophic hands, with thicker ridges on the square and spatulate (see Chapter 4).

Classical palmists believed that finer skin texture denoted a more intellectual, sensitive nature, but this has been proven untrue. Traditionally, the thick-skinned person has been equated with someone who does manual work and is insensitive to the environment. Since it's now known that skin ridges are laid down in the womb, and that the depth of these ridges account for smoothness or seeming roughness, it hardly seems plausible to use an outdated standard. The ridges, as laid down during fetal development, last a lifetime. Contact with abrasive materials may cause roughness and some protective thickening, and callouses may appear from continued tool use, but the ridges themselves don't change.

Some of the most environmentally sensitive, or intellectual people I've met have thick-skinned hands. They can be carpenters or professors, but they can have a reverence for the land and enjoy the outdoors, or be bookish. Nor are people with fine ridges more prone to eschew manual labor. I've seen the hands of poets who have extremely thick skin on the hands, and I've met plumbers with fine ridges and smooth-feeling hands.

The herbal plants echinacea, goldenseal, Oregon grape, chamomile, quince, sage, blackthorn, and comfrey, and plant substances such as aloe vera, avocado, and cucumber, serve as healing and moisturizing skin care ingredients. Products containing alcohol should be avoided, since alcohol dries the skin. For an overnight hand treatment, spread sesame, peanut, or olive oil on the hands and cover with gloves or socks.

PROTECTING THE HANDS

Whether the hands are fine or thick skinned, all need protection from the elements. Normal aging and sun exposure damage the skin's elastic fibers. The production of collagen and elastin, responsible for maintenance of connective and elastic tissues, diminishes. That's why elderly people seem to have soft hands. Skin helps cool the body when temperatures rise by distributing the heat flow in widened blood vessels and by providing a surface for sweat evaporation. When the temperature drops, blood vessels narrow, and sweating lessens. We sweat less as we age, so not as much moisture is trapped on the surface to keep the skin moist.

That's why dermatologists recommend the use of non-scented soaps containing cleansing cream. Scented soaps, especially those containing antiperspirants, dry the skin. Cleansing cream helps hold in moisture. Also oils and moisturizers containing alpha-hydroxy acids (AHAs) help hold moisture in the skin. AHAs are also known as glycolic and lactic acid. Glycolic acid serves to loosen dead skin cells on the surface so that the skin is constantly recycled.

Other measures to protect the hands include washing hands with gentle soaps; increasing humidity in the home, especially during the winter months when drying heat is turned on; wearing protective gloves for dish washing, gardening, and other chores that primarily involve use of the hands; and wearing gloves in cold weather to keep the hands warm.

Fingers are particularly susceptible to frostbite in extreme cold weather and exposure to freezing. Blood vessels narrow too much, and for too long, causing circulation problems, which results in oxygen starvation and tissue death. In case of frostbite, Mary Ann Cooper, M.D., associate professor of emergency medicine at the University of Illinois at Chicago, recommends warming the hands immediately by immersing in warm water or wrapping in warm materials. Avoid rubbing the hands, and don't drink warm beverages or alcohol.

Most commercial skin care products use animal protein, such as collagen or elastin, in their ingredients because they have proven effective in replenishing skin nutrients. Many similar companies, though, offer skin care products free from animal products. They include: CamoCare, Hauschka, Nature's Gate, Skikai, Aubrey Organics, Derma-E, and Jason Natural Cosmetics.

Avoiding Sun Damage

The best protection for normal care of the hands is to keep them out of the sun, especially when a person is young. The effects of early exposure may not show for many years. The ravages of sun damage can be seen by comparing the left hand and lower arm to the right arm and hand. If you drive a car much, with the left hand exposed to the sun shining through the window, you'll notice it is slightly darker and has more freckles or brown spots than the right hand. Hands are one of the most telling signs of age, more so than even the face. Several women I know cover their left arms completely when driving a car. One sixty-year-old artist, a friend, has a line-free face, and could easily pass for someone in her mid-forties. Her hands, however, show the tell-tale signs of age. She had followed a strict regimen of facial skin care throughout her life, she said, but hadn't paid that much attention to her hands.

The sun's ultraviolet rays stimulate the production of melanin, darkening the skin, causing what we know as "suntan." In addition to the threat of skin cancer, UV rays weaken the elastic fibers of the skin, causing a loss of collagen, resulting in looser skin that eventually loses its ability to snap back after stretching. After years of sun exposure, some amounts of collagen can be restored if the hands are covered and protected. Loose skin and loss of collagen are not the only result, though, of sun exposure. It sets the stage for cancerous melanoma, especially on fair-skinned people. It is particularly important to protect the hands because 90 percent of skin cancers occur on parts of the body not usually covered by clothing—the hands, face, ears, and forearms.

Some new research says that exposing young children to the sun may be more dangerous than continued exposure as an adult. If children lived in sunny locales during their early years, the increased risk of melanoma follows them no matter where they eventually reside, according to Thomas Mack, M.D., professor of preventive medicine at the University of Southern California School of Medicine. Even if precautions are taken as adults, their childhood exposure sets the stage for skin problems, such as melanoma, a condition that annually afflicts more than twenty-eight thousand people, and that increases yearly by 4 percent.

Those who spent childhoods in northern states enjoy relative safety from skin melanoma even though they may have spent decades as adults in sunny locales. Those raised as children in sun-belt states, but who lived as adults in northern climates, continued to have a two and a half times greater risk of melanoma, says Mack.

Mack calls the condition a "time bomb" since emphasis has been placed on protection as an adult, with links to depletion of the ozone layer that shields the earth from harmful radiation. "Whatever is happening, is happening early," he says. "It could be that we get 80 percent of our sun exposure as children because we're outside more, or it could be a special susceptibility that sets the process in motion at that earlier age. We just don't know yet." The development of most melanoma requires a long latency period, so the current increase in the deadly skin cancer isn't the result of ozone depletion, according to Mack. "The ozone is bad, but nothing we would see yet in terms of melanoma."

Even though the studies show that the worst effects of sun exposure may occur in childhood, Mack and others nevertheless strongly urge the use of broad-spectrum sunscreens for both children and adults to minimize the sun's deep penetrating UVA rays, and the cancer-promoting UVB rays. Sunscreens should have at least a fifteen or higher Sun Protection Factor (SPF). It's also a good idea to simply keep the skin covered. If you've ever paid much attention to the hands of women past seventy-five, you might notice that the skin opposite the palm contains fewer blemishes than those of their younger counterparts. They were raised in an age when sun worshipping wasn't in vogue, and when wearing gloves was popular.

A condition not related to sun exposure, called "keratolysis," involves an abnormal shedding of skin, usually on the palms of the hands or soles of the feet. It can also be involved with a birth defect, whereby the skin is shed periodically.

THE HANDSHAKE

The handshake can give you first clues to how the person is feeling inwardly, and toward you. If you've ever shaken hands with what you might call, a "wet fish," your observation is probably correct. A limp handshake means the person is either not interested in you, might possess a negative personality, is shy, or is feeling weak at the time. The condition can be temporary.

A firm grip is shown by people with good self-esteem. They are usually outgoing, healthy, and genuinely interested in the other person. If the handshake is too firm and quick, the person may be trying to impress the one whose hand he or she is shaking, or the person may feel restless and hurried.

Sweaty hands can be a sign of nervousness. The body contains about 2 million sweat ducts, with a good portion of them centered in the armpits, the groin, and on the soles of the feet and the palms. Some people have nervous systems that make them prone to display their nervousness with sweaty hands. Others might get an upset stomach, but we wouldn't notice it when shaking their hands.

Many subtleties, such as the texture, color, temperature, and the feel one gets when grasping the hand of another person, are important to the overall health characteristics found in the hands. Such findings draw immediate attention to the inner state of a person, and provide important clues to that person's potential health.

IV

SHAPES OF
THE HANDS

Hands are one of the most magnificent parts of the body. Composed of twenty-seven bones, they have the greatest flexibility of any part of the skeleton. Giving life to the hands are the *palmar aponeurosis*, a connective tissue surrounding the muscles of the palm; *the palmaris longus*, a long, slender muscle of the forearm that flexes the hand; and a hearty blood supply consisting of the palmar metacarpal artery that nourishes the fingers. Also, the ulnar and radial arteries, which are branches of the brachial (the main artery of the upper arm), provide blood to the hands. The ulnar and radial arteries extend beneath the mounts of Luna and Venus in the palm. More than a dozen other veins and arteries serve the hands, so they are well supplied to perform the many tasks we ask of them.

WHY DO WE HAVE PARTICULAR HAND SHAPES?
The basic shape of the hand is determined in the fetus, and by genes inherited from both parents. Similarities between the hands of parents and children and siblings often occur. The following prints (figures 7 and 8), belonging to fourteen-year-old male fraternal twins, Jacob and Joshua Soto, demonstrate the likeness in the hands between siblings,

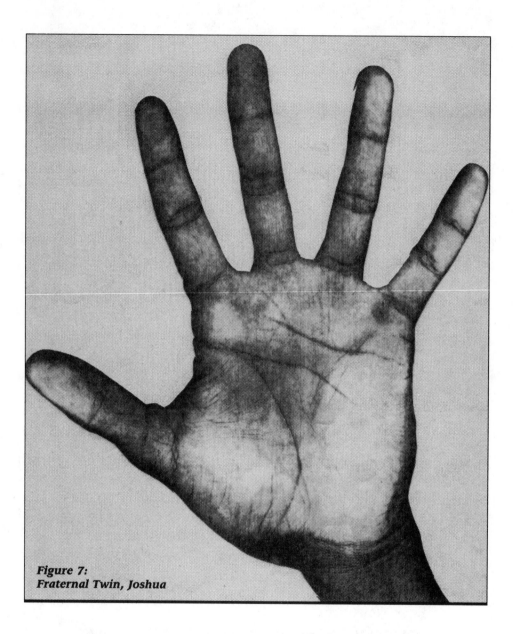

Figure 7:
Fraternal Twin, Joshua

even though they aren't identical twins. Once outside the womb, the hand continues to grow—more in length than breadth through the teens.

Stepping back to prehistorical times, hand shapes were originally partly determined by where and how a person lived. People living in cold climates, such as Eskimos, developed small, squat bodies to minimize body surface areas in order to preserve heat. Smaller body

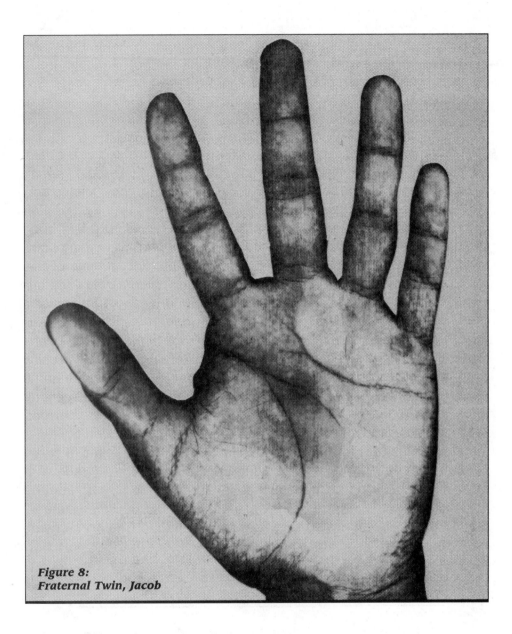

Figure 8:
Fraternal Twin, Jacob

size meant less cold exposure. The hands, too, often exposed to extreme cold, were shorter with squat fingers.

Thus, having long, tapered fingers, which is the ideal in some cultures, is a matter more of race and adaptation to surroundings than a global type hand shape of choice. Because so much of what western societies know about palm reading comes from cultures originating in warmer climates where longer hands and fingers were the norm, an early bias toward particular hand shapes may have developed. That's why each hand must be read on an individual basis.

CLASSICAL AND MODERN HAND SHAPES

Immanuel Kant, as reported in several books on the hand, called hands "the outside brain of man." Ancient palmistry referred to seven types of hand shapes. They were the square, spatulate, conic, elemental, philosophical, psychic, and mixed.

Today, most palm readers have dropped references to the square, short-fingered elemental hand since it smacks of elitism. Or they have switched to more modern terms because identification of some of the ancient hand types were difficult and confusing, such as the "psychic hand." The original psychic hand didn't mean that a person was "psychic" as we refer to it today. It meant "weak." It was identified as being long, flat, and slender. Bearers of this hand could never seem to find their niche in life because of their gentle, dreamy natures, usually accompanied by ill health. The people I've met with this type hand appear to get along as well as anyone else, although they never seem to have much ambition and, perhaps, suffer more than their share of psychosomatic illnesses.

The philosophic hand can still be found, but it is more rare, belonging to, but not limited to, philosophers and spiritual leaders. It falls into the "air hand" category. It is characterized by its length, usually long and tapering in comparison to others in the same culture. It is thick, often with developed finger joints, and a palm covered with many lines. For purposes of this book, I will use the "modern" or "astrological" hand shapes.

A square, or earth, hand is practical, reliable, and realistic. A conic, or water, hand is quick to adapt to new surroundings, and affable. A spatulate, or fire, hand is creative, inventive, and energetic. A pointed, or air, hand is contemplative, idealistic, and sensitive.

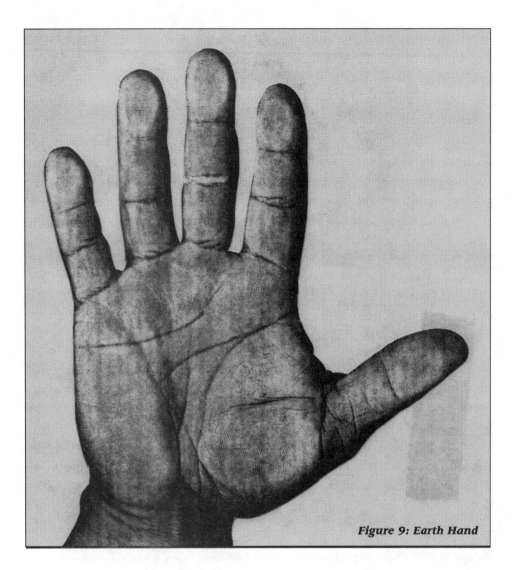

Figure 9: Earth Hand

MODERN AND ASTROLOGICAL HAND SHAPES

These astrological or modern type hand designations mostly deal with the shape of the palm. Generally a person ends up with what is called a "mixed hand," determined by the types of fingertips he or she possesses (see Chapter 6). Thus, people with conic, or "water hands," but with at least some fingertips that are square, have an artistic nature, and are able to cultivate their abilities in the arts through hard work. If they have water hands, plus conic (pointed) fingertips,

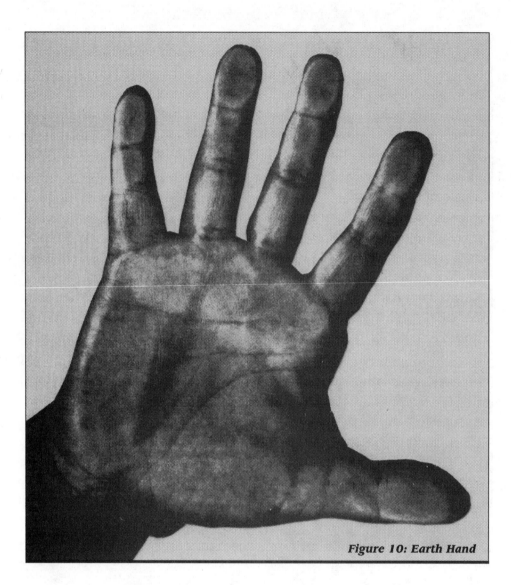

Figure 10: Earth Hand

love of the arts will be a part of their lives, but they won't have the energy to develop their own artistic abilities. If they have spatulate-shaped hands with some conic fingertips, they would be very inventive artistically.

You can determine these overall traits by studying both the shape of the hands and fingertips, and combining the meanings. Also, other features must be taken into consideration, such as elasticity of the palm, texture, color, the lines, and how a person holds his or her hands. No

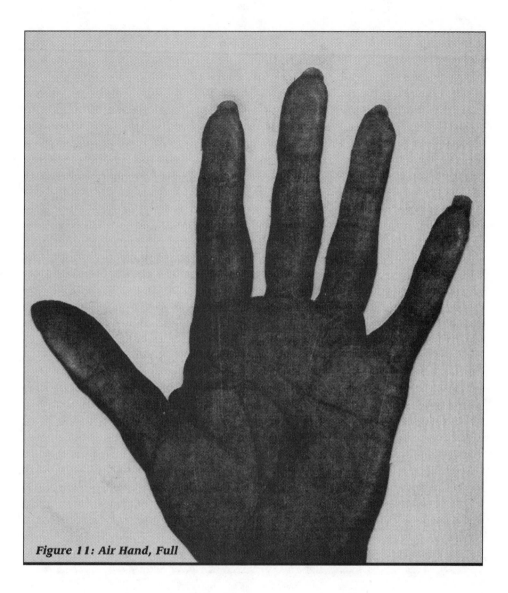

Figure 11: Air Hand, Full

one characteristic by itself tells the story, so it is necessary to study all portions of this book before making determinations about your own or another person's hands. Each section of the book gives an overall view of a particular hand manifestation. Then they must be combined for a complete reading.

The practical square, or "earth," hand is nearly as broad as it is long, and belongs to the hard working individual, whether that work is physical or intellectual.

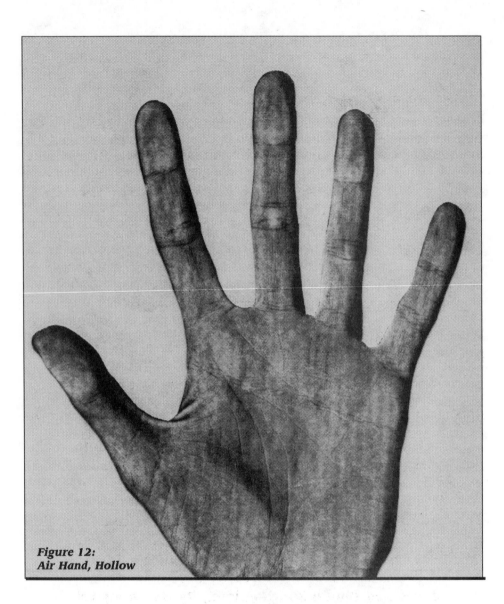

Figure 12:
Air Hand, Hollow

The square hand looks neat and orderly, and the individual will retain some of these characteristics, even if the shape of the fingers differ. He or she can be a conforming individual, especially if the fingers are also square tipped. If any of the fingers are pointed, or spatulated, the person will be far more open-minded, and less conforming. In matters of health, he or she will be more likely to stick to conservative medical treatments, and may, in fact, resent having to go to any sort of doctor. If, however, the person has pointed or spatulated fingertips, he or she might try alternative treatments, but would be very cautious about it.

The elongated and pointed, or air, hand (figures 11 and 12) can also be hard working, especially in intellectual pursuits. These people can be extremely sensitive and idealistic, but if the hand is well padded, they also have a tough inner strength that puts them in touch with the realities of life. They retain philosophic natures, both as students and teachers, and make strong spiritual leaders. When this hand is extremely narrow, though, it weakens the physical fortitude, even though the mind can stay as sharp as ever. If the hand is hollow, with little development of the mounts, their sensitive and idealistic natures become extreme and prevent them from accomplishing much. They become disassociated from reality. They are always concerned with the environment and the world's injustices, but take very little action.

Before trying alternative medical treatments, those with well-developed air hands usually first study the subject thoroughly, and then make a decision. Those with hollow palms are usually easily swayed.

President Clinton has large, air type hands with long, straight fingers, suggesting a contemplative nature not given to quick judgment or decisions. The wide arch between his thumb and finger of Jupiter makes him accepting of new ideas, and his Line of Heart that heads toward Jupiter means he expects a lot from people and can be a hard taskmaster. Former President Bush has a well-developed thumb showing integrity and a logical mind, since the midsection of the thumb is quite long. The knotting joints of presidential candidate Perot's fingers, and square hands bordering on a spatulate shape, indicate an inquisitive nature given to minute details. The tightness of his thumb and its small arch mean he's not very broad-minded.

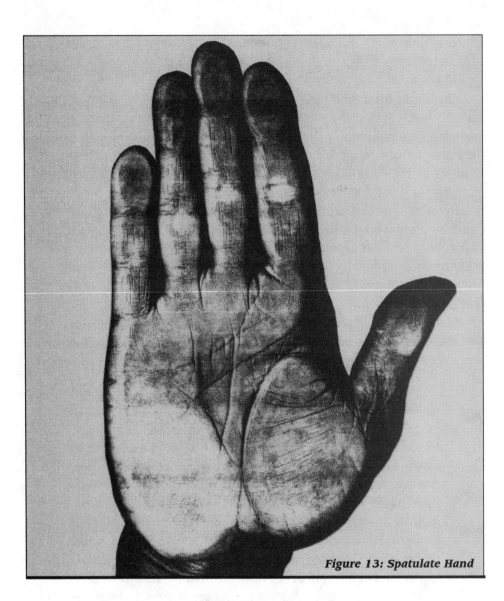

Figure 13: Spatulate Hand

The spatulate shaped, or fire, hand (figure 13) is either wider at the bottom or the top, and tapers to the opposite end of the palm. This is the hand of the creator, the innovator, and inventor. Its shape, as indicated, is like a spatulate. People with these hands are full of ideas and energy, and resent conformity. They are fun, stimulating people to be around. With well-developed mounts, they use their creativity in the arts and sciences. If the widest part of the palm is near the wrist, the person is independent and not

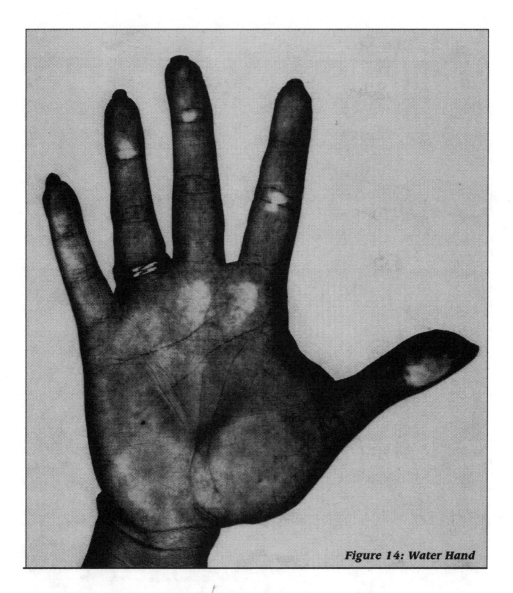

Figure 14: Water Hand

given to working within prescribed perimeters. If the widest part is nearer the fingers, he or she will be more apt to take direction from others—such as a specific assignment from a company boss. When the palms are thin, ideas go up in smoke. Those with fire hands would be likely to try new methods to overcome an illness, or to develop their own techniques.

The conic, or water, hand, identifiable by its tapering, yet well-padded look, belongs to those who put art into their lives—whether they

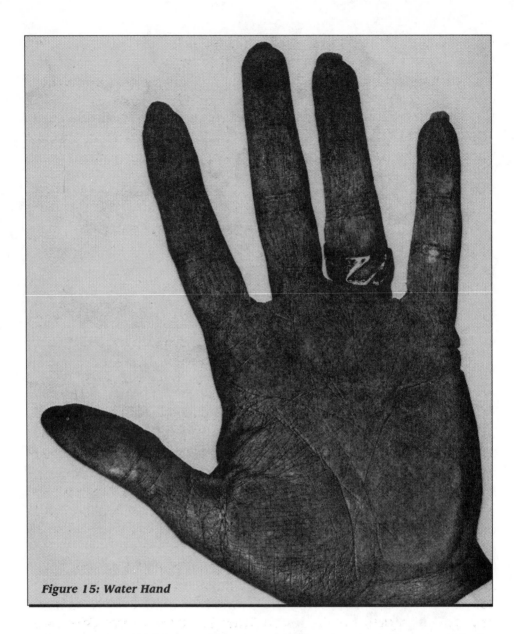

Figure 15: Water Hand

are accountants, carpenters, or engineers. Not necessarily endowed with artistic ability themselves, they, nevertheless, are intuitive and have a good grasp of the artistic side of life. In combination with square tipped fingers, they can become artists, but often have to force themselves to "get down to business." Conic hands usually are well padded, especially the Mount of Venus, as if to absorb all they encounter. People with water hands tend to be emotional, although many hold their feelings inside. Some, depending on other markings on the hands, are ripe candidates for alternative medical practices because they are easily swayed by others. They might be prone to try unproven health practices.

Water and air hands are sometimes confused with one another. The difference exists in the gentler look of the water hand. The air hand, though shaped similar, and if not hollow, looks much stronger than the water hand.

HAND SHAPES IN RELATION TO BODY TYPE

Three main body types are recognized by scientists, although other categories exist within these three shapes.

- O Ectomorph, pertains to someone with a fragile, slender body shape.
- O Endomorph, is characterized by a large trunk and thighs, with a soft and round look to the overall body.
- O Mesomorph bodies have prominent muscles and bones with long arms and legs.

More often than not, I've found that particular hand shapes accompany certain body types. Ectomorphs and endomorphs tend more often to have air- or water- (pointed) type hands, and occasionally, square hands. Mesomorphs frequently have square (earth hands), or spatulate (fire) hands. Also, heavily jointed fingers are more often found on mesomorphs, with a greater proportion of ectomorphs and endomorphs having smooth joints.

Sometimes when I'm studying palms from prints alone and have never met the person, I can visualize what he or she looks like, and I don't think it's psychic. I believe the multitude of clues in the hand itself helps paint this picture of the person. When I read from prints alone, I do need to know the person's age, and which hand is dominant. This also helps complete the picture.

FOUR PALM CATEGORIES

In classical palmistry, the palm is separated into four categories, or quadrants. The lower portion deals with earthly matters, the upper

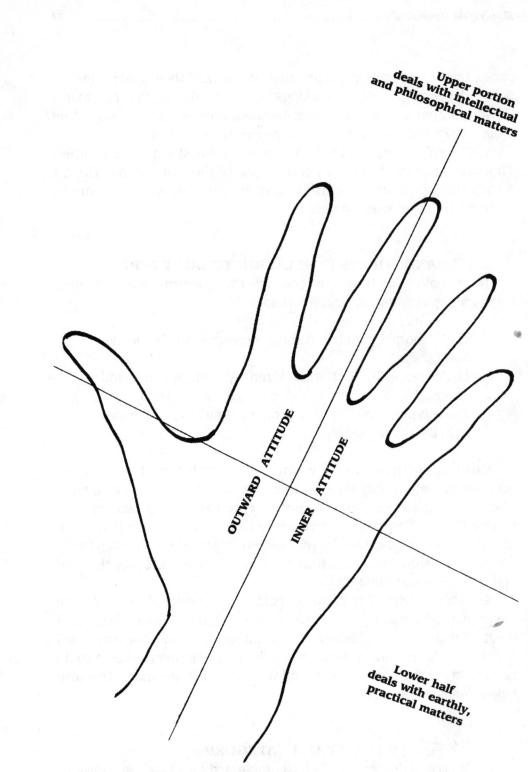

Upper portion
deals with intellectual
and philosophical matters

OUTWARD ATTITUDE

INNER ATTITUDE

Lower half
deals with earthly,
practical matters

Figure 16: Four Palm Categories, or Quadrants

portion with the intellect and philosophic disposition. The ulnar, or percussion side of the hand (Luna), containing the little finger, represents the inner way we deal with the world and our lives, and the radial, or thumb side of the hand (Venus), shows our outward attitude toward life and other people.

For example, the lower portion, which contains the bulk of the Mount of Venus, deals with passion, or the human earth nature. The upper portion usually contains the lines of Heart and Head that correspond to the intellectual nature of the person, whether that be philosophy or love. The side of the hand containing the Mount of Luna deals with a person's imaginative, transcending qualities—important attributes in coloring one's view of the world. The thumb side of the hand, contains Venus and the thumb, as well as the Finger of Jupiter, all which relate to how one deals with others. The quadrants provide a ready guide to the interpretation of the signs and markings contained within their spheres of influence.

MEDICAL CONDITIONS AND HAND SHAPES

Several chronic conditions or diseases show symptoms in the hands, and some interfere with their use. Surgery and physical therapy are sometimes used in treatment.

Carpal tunnel syndrome is much in the news today because of its increase, due in part to computer use. As many as 35 percent of people whose hobbies or jobs require repetitive hand and wrist movements can be affected. The syndrome is caused by pressure from swollen tissue around the tendons on the middle nerve that goes through the wrist in the area of the carpal tunnel. It can cause swelling, tumors, rheumatoid arthritis, or affect the nerves that serve the palm and thumb side of the hand. It creates burning, tingling, and aching that can spread to the forearm and shoulder, and can lead to muscle deterioration. Eventually, paralysis can result in the affected thumb and fingers.

It was once thought to be a condition mostly affecting women over forty, or pregnant women. Today, though, it causes major problems for men and women who continually use their hands in controlled, repetitive movements, such as computer or tool use. Treatments consist of splinting, physical therapy, anti-inflammation medications, and steroid injections, and are effective up to 80 percent of the time. For the other nearly 20 percent, surgery is required.

Boonmee Chunprapaph, associate professor of orthopedics, University of Illinois at Chicago, says one of the best protections for computer users is to wear pads or splints to keep the wrist from flexing. Changing body posture at work, learning to hold the hands so that the wrists don't lean on anything while typing into a computer, or learning how to use tools differently can also be helpful.

Dupuytren's contracture is a progressive and painless thickening and tightening of tissue under the skin of the palm. It causes the ring and little fingers (Apollo and Mercury) to pull toward the center of the palm. It was once thought to be caused by heavy alcohol consumption, but that has yet to be proven. It may be hereditary.

Acromegalia and Marfan's syndrome: With the disease acromegalia, caused by a pituitary gland tumor, certain parts of the body grow inordinately large, including he hands. Marfan's syndrome, an inherited condition, related to excess bone length, may also show up first in hands that look excessively long and slender.

Sickle cell anemia can cause the hands to swell, limiting joint movement. It is caused by painful swelling of the hand's soft tissues. The disease is an incurable blood disorder that attacks the red blood cells which can create blood clots, fever, enlargement of the spleen, and weakness.

☞ ────────────────────────────

An exaggerated angle on the thumb side of the hand at the bottom of the palm, coupled with a puffy Mount of Venus in the lower portion of the mount, can indicate a propensity toward alcoholism. When the entire mount is well developed, and the thumb side angular, it indicates a good sense of rhythm and is often found on the hands of musicians.

────────────────────────────

V

THE FINGERS

Much about a person's personality can be determined by the shape, size, and placement of the fingers and the thumb. How the fingers lean toward one another, and their very structure, provide information about the person's inherent traits, and how that person makes use of his or her capabilities.

MAKEUP OF THE FINGERS

Fingers are made up of a metacarpal bone and three joints, or bony hinges sometimes called phalanges. Usually we refer to the number of fingers as four on each hand, but some include the thumb as a finger, although it has one less bone, or joint. Physicians count the "digits" of the hand from one to five, beginning with the thumb. Palmistry has ascribed other names to these digits: one is the thumb; two is the Finger of Jupiter; three is the Finger of Saturn; four is the Finger of Apollo; and five is the Finger of Mercury.

Each finger represents certain traits or influences in the person's life, and each one of the three sections, or phalanges, of the fingers represents a spiritual, mental, or physical trait, according to ancient palmistry. The thumb has only two phalanges, each representing a personality characteristic. Some palmists, though, consider the lower portion, or Mount of Venus, as one of three thumb phalanges.

Observing the shape and characteristics of the fingers and thumbs give clues to the person's personality, and, in some cases, his or her health. Although medical scientists do not traditionally ascribe personality to the size and shapes of the fingers, they do recognize other hand and finger conditions, some of which palm readers have noted for years, such as the finding that individuals with Down's syndrome often lack the topmost phalange on their fifth (Mercury or little) finger.

THE SENSE OF TOUCH

New studies of the brain might help clarify why some long-established tenants of palmistry work. Exploring the sense of touch through modern technology shows that the tips of the fingers, and the tongue, contain more sense receptors (or density of receptor units) than any other part of the body. Thus, a blind person can "read" through the sense of touch.

Scientific maps of the brain indicate that the hand, particularly the fingertips, take up more cortical space than their size indicates. Thus, the hands and fingers take up more brain area than the legs and feet, which are far larger. Blindfold yourself and try identifying objects with the bottoms of your feet. Then try it with your fingertips.

Our fingertips also assist visual image. Richard Restak, M.D., writes in *The Brain* that "when you identify a penny by holding it out of sight and rolling it between your fingers, activating your skin receptors has made it possible to form a visual image. Clearly, receptors for touch and manipulation must somehow be combined in the brain with visual receptors to provide this unity in perception." Thus, the hand/finger connection to particular portions of the brain has been established (also see Chapter 1).

Heat, cold, vibration, and the difference in light and heavy pressure are easily determined by touch since the fingers contain more than a million nerve receptors. With touch, receptors are triggered, sending a signal to a nerve, into the spinal column and finally to the brain. Lack of sensation in the fingers is caused by nerve damage, although occasionally it is the result of damage to the receptors.

THE THUMB

The thumb is considered by many palmists to be the key to a person's personality, and has drawn the interest of all segments of society and disciplines. Isaac Newton said of the thumb: "In the absence of any other proof, the thumb alone would convince me of God's existence."

So well known is the idea of the thumb's importance that Karl Ritter, a character in Mark Twain's *Life on the Mississippi*, tells of a fortune-telling sequence involving only his thumb. And it's not surprising that Mark Twain, himself, once had his palm read by Cheiro, a noted palm reader of the early twentieth century.

Human beings, among some other primates, are endowed with an opposable thumb, able to coordinate its use with other fingers. It is credited by anthropologists as one of the reasons for human advancement since it enabled our ancestors to manipulate tools and weapons.

It contains only two phalanges, although the mount lying at its base, the mount of Venus, can be considered a third phalange. The elevation of the mount of Venus (thenar eminence in medical terms), is mostly due to the strong muscles in this area that control the thumb. That is why many palm readers touch the lower portion (Venus) of the thumb. It tells them instantly by touch the strength and robustness of the individual whom they are reading.

Thumb Movements

Movements of the thumb also give clues to a person's mental state. An early observation by physicians indicated that a child learns to use his forefinger and thumb simultaneously when his ego is developing. Thus long dominating thumbs and index fingers are associated with strong egos, and undeveloped, short thumbs indicate weak egos.

An acquaintance once told me of her uncle, who, in his fifties, deteriorated mentally to the point he was placed in an institution. She noted during this period of deterioration that he began holding his thumb inside his hand in a fist as if he were trying to hide it. During his stay in the institution as he began getting treatment, the thumb occasionally made its way outside the hand. By the time he was released, the thumb was no longer hidden inside the clenched hand. Individuals who are not having serious mental problems like the woman's uncle, but who might be having temporary difficulties,

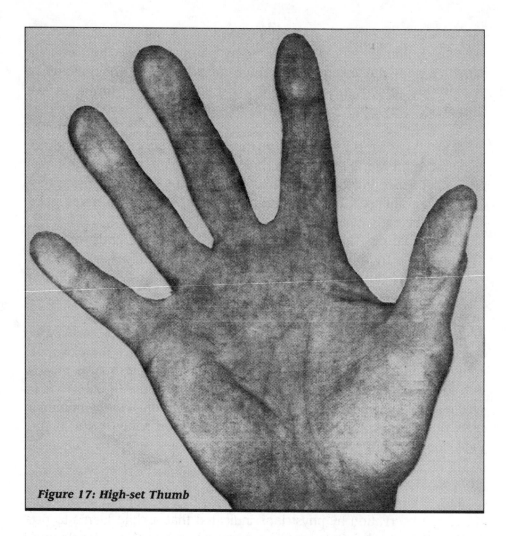

Figure 17: High-set Thumb

often hold their thumbs inside the clenched fist. Often, when mulling over a problem, we will place our thumbs in this position and rest our elbows on a table or desk with the thumb side of the hand pressed to our lips.

Shapes of the Thumb

Palmists consider large, well-shaped thumbs as an indication of energy, leadership ability, high-minded goals, and strength of character. To determine whether or not a thumb is large or small, one must consider the length of the other fingers. If a person has short, stubby

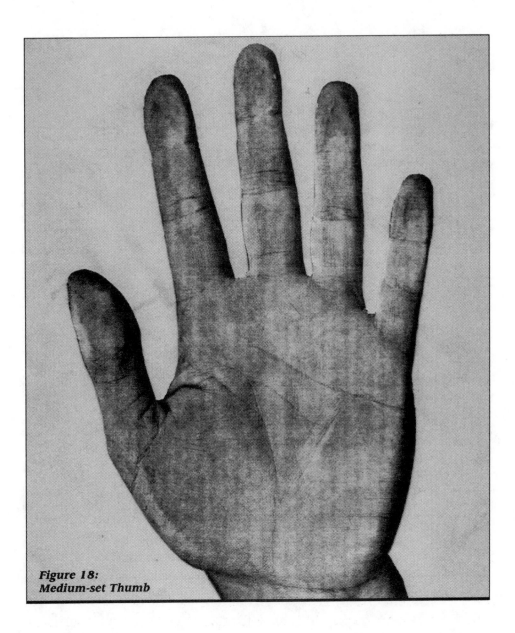

Figure 18:
Medium-set Thumb

fingers, his or her thumb is naturally going to appear shorter when compared to those of a long-fingered individual. Also, if the thumb is set low to the bottom of the palm, it won't seem as long as one that juts out higher up. So when determining the length of the thumb, the entire hand must be taken into consideration and judged on its own merit and not in comparison with someone else's thumb.

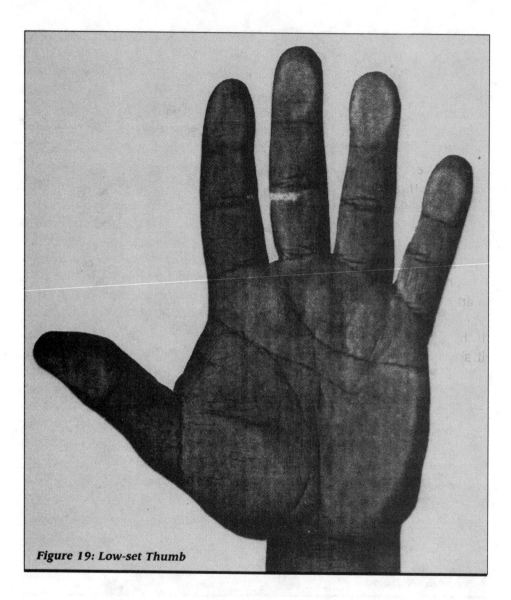

Figure 19: Low-set Thumb

Unless a thumb is excessively weak and little, I don't pay too much attention to length because I've seen short thumbs on too many brilliant people—from neuroscientists to artists, and from bright homemakers to knowledgeable laborers.

The placement of the thumb, whether it sits high, medium, or low on the side of the hand, provides information on how an individual relates to other people. It also tells a great deal about the person's character.

High-set thumbs that jut from the middle of the mount of Venus, indicate stubbornness, and sometimes shyness.

High set on a rigid hand indicates low self-esteem, and high set on a flexible hand indicates strong will power.

Medium-set thumbs can take on the qualities of both low- and high-set thumbs, usually more closely resembling the characters of the high-set individual.

Low-set thumbs, which begin closer to the wrist, and usually don't extend to the first joint of the index finger, belong to those who like being around people. If the thumb is also long, they like the center of attention, yet at the same time, make wonderful hosts.

Other Thumb Shapes

The shape and placement of the thumb on the hand also give palmists clues to a person's personality and temperament.

Long tapering thumbs indicate an intellectual and curious nature. If this long thumb is set low, beginning close to the bottom of the hand, it shows warm heartedness and refinement. When narrow and waist-like, it indicates spiritual sensitivity.

Thick, as well as large, indicates materialism, and independence. Extreme thickness, though, shows coarseness and tactlessness.

The medium-sized thumb shows balance between the spiritual, intellectual, and materialistic nature. It also indicates a person who balances the use of his or her head and heart to make decisions.

Short thumbs indicate cautiousness and uncontrolled emotion. If it is short and blunt, the person can be fussy, nosy, and quarrelsome. Short and thick, it can lead to violent outbursts and obstinacy. People with extremely short thumbs, taking hand size and the length of other fingers into consideration, tend to be ruled by emotion.

Murderer's thumb (so called), short, and shaped like a club, or bulb, was once believed to contain such negative energy that it would lead to murder. Today, it is considered the sign of people who have flash tempers. They may seem like very easygoing people, but if aroused, they are blinded by their passion and negative energy. Under control, though, they can direct their energy toward worthwhile pursuits. Too, bulbous thumbs can be an indication of hyperthyroidism, or poor circulation.

Rigid thumbs show strong will and conformity. They often use this will, though, to overcome illness.

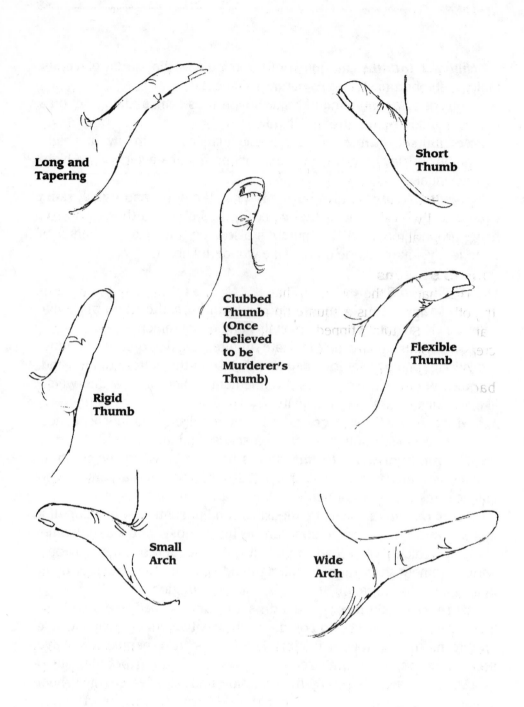

Long and Tapering

Short Thumb

Clubbed Thumb (Once believed to be Murderer's Thumb)

Flexible Thumb

Rigid Thumb

Small Arch

Wide Arch

Figure 20: Other Thumb Shapes

Flexible thumbs belong to the more gregarious person. Yet, when the thumb is too flexible, the person may allow an illness to overtake him or her. When the thumb is flexible on the dominant hand, but stiff on the nondominant one, the person is not really as open as he or she appears to be.

Wide arches between the thumb and Finger of Jupiter belong to nonjudgmental, open-minded individuals.

Small arches belong to those who show more caution when confronted with change and when meeting new people. Yet, they make staunch, loyal friends.

Thumb Sections

The shape of the thumb tip has double the meaning that it does on the other digits. Thus a square tip promises stamina and the ability for hard work. Spatulate tipped, and the person is extremely inventive and creative. Pointed, and it lends itself to artistic endeavors.

Arched tipped thumbs, whereby the first joint of the thumb arches back radically, is found on the hands of people who are innately concerned with the welfare of others. They get along well with people, and make good caregivers.

Thumb Phalanges

The thumb's phalanges indicate clues to a person's demeanor. Study them carefully, as they can reveal much.

The first phalange (tip) represents willpower. When it is longer than the second phalange, the individual uses that power to solve problems.

The second phalange (lower portion of the thumb) represents logic. When it is the longest of the two, logic is the person's forte. Balance is seen when the two phalanges are equal.

Scientists in the late 1930s reported several cases of men with three phalanges on the thumb. One case involved two brothers who also displayed poorly developed mounts of Venus. The mother also had three phalanges. The condition is believed to be related to polydactyly, a hereditary trait resulting in extra numbers of fingers and toes.

Special Markings

Often, special markings exist on the thumb. If one knows what to look for, they can reveal fascinating character traits.

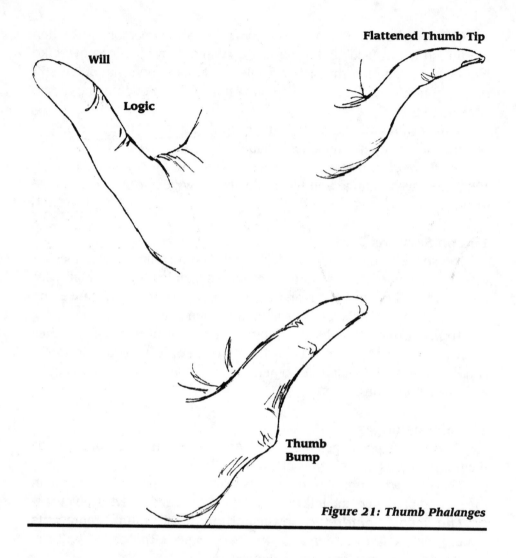

Figure 21: Thumb Phalanges

A flattened thumb tip, on the palm side of the hand, starting about opposite the bottom of the fingernail and continuing to the tip, is the sign of a person who has a problem completing projects he or she starts. This includes completing a full regimen of medications prescribed by a physician. The individual might take it for a few days, and then "taper off." Unfortunately, not completing a prescribed regimen of drugs for treatment is a major problem. We tend to believe, and sometimes with good cause, that drugs are overprescribed in some cases. Yet studies show that 15 percent of patients do not take a full course of a prescribed drug, rendering it

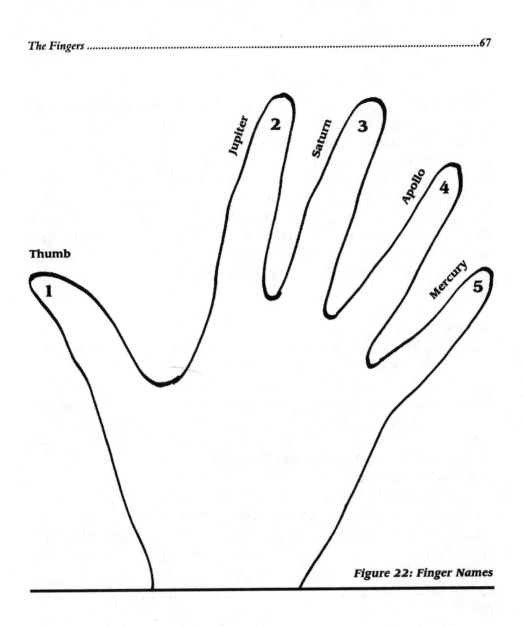

Figure 22: Finger Names

ineffective since it often takes a few days or even weeks for some drugs to be beneficial.

The thumb bump, sometimes called the "philosopher's bump," found on the lowest joint of the thumb, next to Venus, belongs to philosophers, religious personages, and those who seriously study metaphysics.

NAMES OF THE FINGERS

Each finger has a personality of its own. Its length, thickness, sections, and bend tell something about the person's personality, character, and mental health.

An individual can hold his or her hands in such a position as to make one finger seem longer than another, and this gives a palm reader telling clues. Of importance, though, is how the person holds these fingers in a relaxed position. Thus, if, say, the Finger of Jupiter (index finger) is nearly as long as Apollo (ring finger), it has a particular meaning (likes to be in control). But if a person tries hard enough, he or she can reverse this long-short alignment. Yet, it won't show the true nature of the individual because the alignment is not the natural position. Direct links to the brain exist to the fingers—so the normal, relaxed position tells us the inherent thought patterns of the person.

Mercury

The little finger, or Finger of Mercury, is associated with the muscles in the ulnar side of the hand, particularly the Mount of Luna (hypothenar area in medical terms). Mercury is associated with communication, business sense, and science. A long Finger of Mercury (nearly touching the first phalange or joint) indicates public speaking abilities. Ministers, politicians, and actors often have this formation. A short little finger denotes difficulty with communication skills, especially if the little finger curls toward the palm.

When long and unbent on the dominant hand, but curled on the nondominant one, the person may appear to be expressive, but rarely reveals much. Its association to health is found in the second phalange, according to palmists. When this section is longer than the other phalanges, it indicates an ability to practice the medical sciences.

Apollo

When the ring finger, Apollo, is well shaped and rising slightly above the first joint of the middle finger, it portends creativity in the arts. Exceptionally long (longer than the index finger) marks the daredevil. Longer yet (as long as Saturn), shows the compulsive gambler. If it is the same length as Jupiter, it indicates a person well balanced in money matters.

Saturn

Large, well-shaped Saturn (middle) fingers denote individuals with a keen moral sense. If it is exceptionally long and thick, though, it can indicate a depressive nature. If the finger is slightly bent inward, the person is overly cautious. If crooked, the person can be morbid. If it is stiff and leans backward on the nondominant hand, yet is supple and curves with the rest of the fingers on the dominant hand, the individual has a hidden agenda. He or she may appear to be nonjudgmental and accepting of the ideas being put forth, when, in truth, he or she is constantly making mental notes of disagreement.

Jupiter

Lengthy Jupiter fingers show good self-esteem, and how the person relates to the outside world. Well-developed Jupiters possess leadership ability when other markings are well formed. If the finger is excessively long, the person can have an authoritarian nature. A crooked Jupiter finger indicates lack of integrity. When bent inward, it shows extreme caution.

OTHER ELEMENTS OF THE FINGERS

Certain characteristics of the fingers taken as a whole offer immediate and observable information about an individual's temperament. For instance, when the hand is held up, observe the spacing between the fingers. Held close together, the person is cautious and private. When they are wide apart, the person is generous and open to new experiences.

Leaning Toward One Another

There are certain mental and emotional signs that can be read simply from observing the ways that the fingers lean toward each other:

> ○ When the fingers are straight, and not leaning toward another one, the temperament is balanced.
> ○ When the fingers lean toward the percussion side of the hand (towards Mercury) the person is governed by emotions and instinct. He or she tends to be extroverted.
> ○ Fingers leaning toward Saturn indicate a serious, contemplative nature.
> ○ Fingers leaning toward Jupiter indicate leadership ability.
> ○ If the Jupiter finger, even though long, leans toward Saturn, it negates the leadership ability. Leaning far away from Saturn, it shows independence.

Spaces Between Fingers

Likewise, the spaces between fingers often reveal much amount a person's character:

    ○ Wide spaces between all the fingers indicate openness, extroversion, and a quick mind.
    ○ A wide space between the thumb and Jupiter belongs on the hand of a generous, independent, and friendly person.
    ○ A wide space between Apollo and Mercury, especially if a ring is worn on Mercury, indicates a love of independence.

Length of Fingers

The length of the fingers provide clues about a person's demeanor and makeup:

    ○ Short fingers are quick to action. Short, strong fingers indicate an emotionally sturdy person who could be quite

Figure 23: Forms of the Fingers

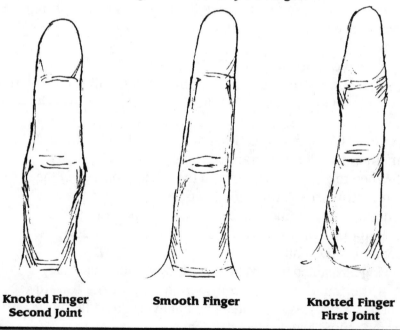

Knotted Finger　　　　　**Smooth Finger**　　　　　**Knotted Finger**
Second Joint　　　　　　　　　　　　　　　　　　　**First Joint**

tenacious in the face of illness. He or she would simply never give up or in.

○ Long fingers are more contemplative. They cherish self-control, but can be wounded by the harshness of others. When the fingers are thin, as well as long, they are masters of intellectual thought and control.

Finger sacrifices have been employed throughout the world. Prehistorical cave art depicts many hand prints with mutilated fingers. Among American plains Indians, offerings of fingers and joints were given to obtain prowess in war, or during visionary fasts.

Forms of the Fingers

Surprisingly, even details as specific as the forms of the fingers reveal interesting information:

○ Smooth fingers are ruled by inspiration and intuition. They are quick to act in a crisis, and when faced with an illness, take quick, positive action. No time is to be wasted.

○ Those with heavily jointed fingers tend toward contemplation. They must think things through carefully before taking action.

○ When the joint is more pronounced on the first phalange (closest to the fingertip) the person can appear to be nosey and interfering. The knotty second joint belongs on the hands of analytical individuals. They are more curious than nosey.

Flexible or Stiff Fingers

Much to a palmist's delight, the flexibility or stiffness of a person's finger reveals much about a person's emotional and mental health:

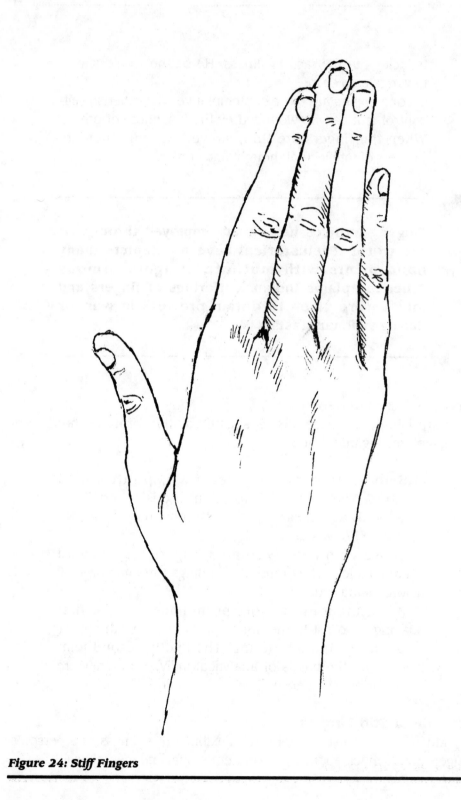

Figure 24: Stiff Fingers

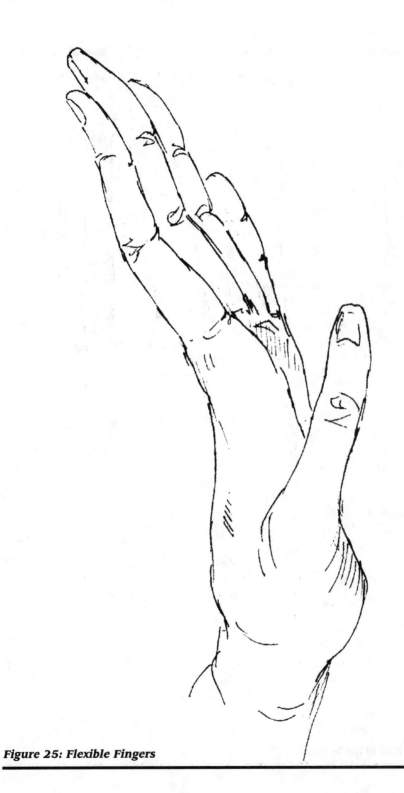

Figure 25: Flexible Fingers

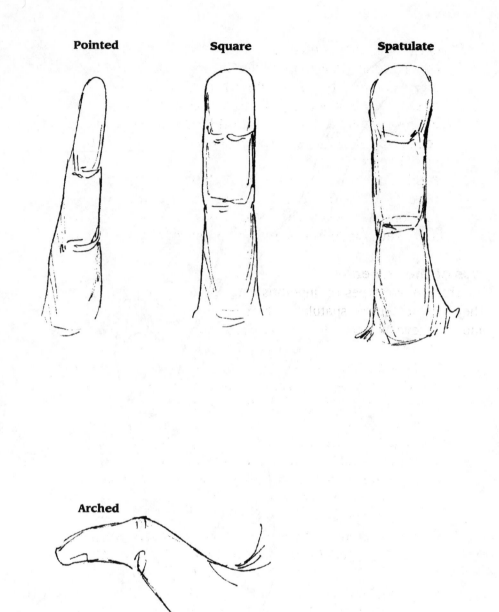

Pointed **Square** **Spatulate**

Arched

Figure 26: Tips of the Fingers

○ Flexible fingers that bend backwards easily are found on outgoing, sharing individuals. They would be more likely to try alternative health remedies. When the fingers are excessively flexible, though, they are too easily swayed, and are gullible to charlatanism. Moderately flexible fingers won't bend back much further than 45 degrees.

○ Stiff fingers belong to stoic people with vast reservoirs of energy. They are hesitant to try new ideas, relationships, or activities. They would be more reluctant to try new, or alternative medical practices.

Tips of the Fingers

Three major types of fingertips exist in the ancient art of palmistry. They are the square, spatulate, and conic (pointed or rounded) shapes, and each reveals something unique about the individual:

○ Pointed (conic fingertips) belong to the idealistic person. They also indicate a love of the arts and, when combined with other spatulate or square fingertips, show the potential for artistic ability.

○ Square-tipped fingers belong on the hands of hard-working individuals who are loyal and steadfast.

○ Spatulate-shaped fingertips are found on the hands of creative, imaginative people. Many inventors have this fingertip shape.

○ A combination of fingertips shows adaptability, and often adds strength to a person's hand. For example, a person with a conic hand and mostly conic fingers would possess idealism and a love of the arts, but lack the energy available from having a few conic or spatulate fingertips.

The shapes of the fingers are mitigated by the shape of the fingertips. Thus, a person with jointed fingers and conic fingertips would think through problems and come to realistic conclusions. Square tips on knotty fingers would act more impulsively, even after taking time to contemplate a situation. The person with smooth joints and square-tipped fingertips would act on impulse, and if the tips were conic he or she might become irritable at being inconvenienced by a lack of energy in the face of illness.

When studying the shape of the hand, the fingertips are always taken into consideration, as they add information about the shape of the hand.

PHALANGES OF THE FINGERS

The phalanges, or three sections of the fingers separated by the joints, often are overlooked when reading the palm. However, they offer clues to established traits that influence an individual's outlook on life, and what he or she expects in return:

> ○ The first section, or phalange, above the first joint of the finger and comprised of the fingertip, involves the intellectual and intuitive nature of the person.
> ○ The second section involves organization and practicality.
> ○ The third section, closest to the palm, deals with vitality, work ethic, and dependability.

The longer of these sections is a central force in the person's life.

Jupiter Phalanges

First phalange: Good judgment and intuition is shown on a long first phalange. If thick, it shows egotism, and when thin, the person is adept at controlling others.

Second phalange: A long second phalange belongs on the hand of a person who is well balanced when it comes to material possessions. Short, and it shows a tendency toward sluggishness. A thick second phalange belongs on the person who loves luxury, and if thin, ambition.

Third phalange: A proud, yet sometimes controlling, nature is shown with a long third phalange. Short, and a stubborn acceptance to life reigns. If this third phalange is excessively thick, the person can be greedy, and if thin, he or she is idealistic.

Saturn Phalanges

First phalange: When the first phalange is the longest of the three, the person can be devoutly religious, or superstitious. If the first phalange is extremely short, the person is easily manipulated by others.

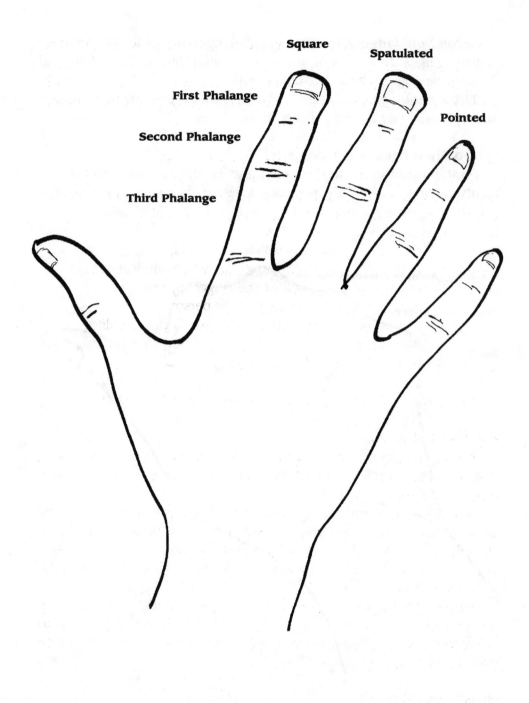

Figure 27: Three Basic Fingertip Shapes and Phalanges

Second phalange: A long second phalange belongs to the gardener. He or she likes the outdoors and love growing things. A short second phalange belongs to the distrustful person.

Third phalange: A long third phalange indicates a loving, sensitive nature. A short one means conservatism.

Apollo Phalanges

First phalange: If the first phalange is longest, love for art and beauty abounds. If short, the person ignores artistic creativity.

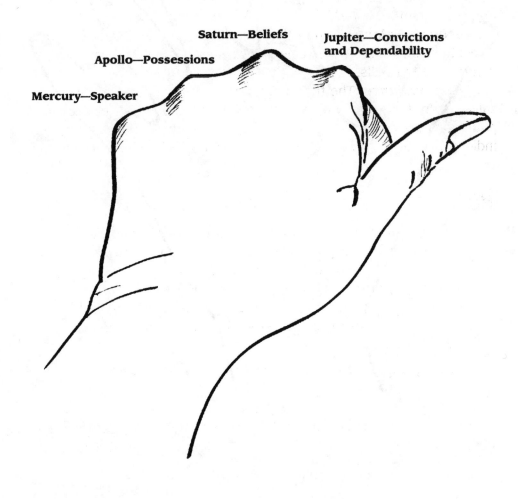

Figure 28: Major Characteristics of Knuckles

Second phalange: When the second phalange is longer than the other two, the person is intellectually gifted in the arts. If short, it shows a lack of fresh ideas.

Third phalange: A third long phalange indicates the desire and energy to work toward artistic achievement. When short, the energy will be lacking.

Mercury Phalanges

First phalange: If the first phalange is long, it shows good communication and intuitive skills. When short, the person has difficulty expressing him- or herself.

Second phalange: When the second phalange is longest of the three, the aptitude is for medicine and science. If short, the person lacks communication skills.

Third phalange: The third phalange, if long, indicates the natural salesperson. If short, the person is passive, but honest. When the third phalanges on two or more of the fingers are thick and puffy, it can indicate allergies to particular foods the person is eating.

Rings worn on the thumbs signify stubbornness; on the little finger, independence; on the pointing finger, dominance; on the middle finger, love of solitude; and when worn on what is known as the ring finger, a need to belong to someone. People who wear numerous rings on their fingers lack self-esteem.

KNUCKLES

The knuckles separating the second and third phalanges also tell something about the person's character. To observe these signs, make a fist. The most prominent knuckle stands for a major character trait:

○ A large Jupiter knuckle shows strong convictions and dependability.

○ Saturn as the most outstanding, indicates the person

who will stand up for his or her beliefs at all cost.
○ A pronounced Apollo knuckle means the person is attached to his or her possessions and will protect them.
○ A significant Mercury knuckle belongs on the hand of a public speaker.

MEDICAL OBSERVATIONS

Many diseases manifest themselves in the fingers, or give signs of impending medical conditions. Some are present at birth and are genetically linked.

Arthritis

One of the most obvious diseases to show on the fingers is arthritis, since it is a joint disease marked by pain and swelling. Of the more than one hundred types of arthritis, osteoarthritis, rheumatoid, and gout are the most common. Swelling of the knuckles at the base of the fingers is an early sign of arthritis, according to Eugene Scheimann, M.D., ninety-three, who, at the time I interviewed him in 1990, was still practicing and using palmistry in diagnosis. Scheimann published many pamphlets on the connection between hand psychology and health, and authored *Dr. Scheimann's Better Health Through Palmistry*, published nearly fifty years ago.

Osteoarthritis involves tissue changes that can result in bone tissue cysts. Cartilage breaks down and no longer cushions the joints. Also, small pieces of bone and cartilage can loosen and get trapped inside the joint, causing additional pain. The hands are frequently the first noticeable part of the body affected.

Rheumatoid arthritis is an autoimmune disease that results in the body rejecting its own tissue. The membranes lining the joints become inflamed, which causes swelling and thickening of the joints. Rheumatoid arthritis most commonly affects the joints of the wrists, hands, and feet. Researchers have recently discovered a genetic connection to the disease.

Medical science offers many treatments now for arthritis, a disease that afflicted our earliest ancestors. Because arthritis is one of those diseases that frequently involves spontaneous remission for weeks, months, or years, it is an easy target for unproven, quack products. Victims pay good money for "cures" believing it will work for them, when in reality the cure involves routine spontaneous remission.

I use caution when dealing with an issue like palmistry and health because it is not in the purview of any palm reader to offer any sort of "cure." I once met a prominent medical surgeon who was testifying in court during the trial of another man accused (and found guilty) of using unproven cancer treatments on his patients. The surgeon himself, in his forties, was suffering the ravages of arthritis and was losing the ability to perform surgery. He was devastated, and had himself tried an unproven arthritic treatment administered by the man on trial—with disastrous results. He cried when talking about his gullibility and how the unproven treatment had worsened his hands.

Diabetes

Observation of the hands, particularly the fingers, is being used to predict which victims of childhood diabetes are most likely to develop dangerous side effects of the disease such as eye and kidney problems brought about by damage to small blood vessels. Researcher Jane H. Silverstein, M.D., of the University of Florida College of Medicine, says the complications are more likely to develop if the children have stiff joints caused by thickened connective tissue around those joints. Those with these stiffened joints have an 83 percent risk of damage to their blood vessels after sixteen years of diabetes, with the danger at 25 percent if the fingers move freely. No cause for this difference in flexibility has thus far been found.

Peptic Ulcer

In the 1940s, one noted medical doctor said he observed that the hands of patients with peptic ulcers are long and graceful looking, with especially long fingers, and that they move about constantly. He believed this constant motion belied their nervous and worrying disposition. Recent medical studies, though, indicate that peptic ulcers are caused by a bacterium that can be eradicated by antibiotics, and are not caused by nervous temperaments.

The studies also indicate that a good percentage of people have the bacteria that causes ulcers in their digestive tracts, yet don't become afflicted. Perhaps the mind/body connection, though, has something to do with susceptibility.

Clubbed Fingers

Clubbed fingers can indicate some forms of heart disease, long-term lung disease, cirrhosis of the liver, colitis, and long-term dysentery.

Hyperthyroidism, a condition marked by nervousness, loss of weight, or an increase in appetite, tremors, and fatigue also causes this full and fleshy finger appearance.

Birth Defects

Symphalangia is an inherited condition marked by stiff fingers and toes joined together in a webbed effect. The term, palmature, is also a medical term used for webbed fingers. Syndactyly is another form of birth defect where fingers or toes grow together, sometimes forming a webbed effect.

VI

FINGERPRINT AND RIDGE PATTERNS

Scientists throughout the world are studying dermal ridge patterns on the mounts of the palms and tips of the fingers (fingerprints), as markers for predetermined behavioral traits, chronic illnesses, and genetic abnormalities. The modern studies, called "dermatoglyphics," was coined in about 1926. The term is comprised of derma, meaning skin, and glyphe, meaning curve. The study of dermatoglyphics is an exacting science involving precise measurements and dermal ridge counts. What is presented in this book is a survey of what has been and is being uncovered by medical scientists.

THE BEGINNINGS OF DERMATOGLYPHIC STUDIES

Although hundreds of dermatoglyphics studies at major universities now take place, many are based on earlier scientific studies in the early 1940s. Observation and theories by medical professionals and palmists alike however, have abounded for centuries, picking up momentum in the late 1800s and early 1900s.

In the late nineteenth and early twentieth centuries, several early dermatoglyphic pioneers, including Francis Galton, Harris Hawthorne Wilder, Inez Whipple-Wilder, Heinrich Poll, and Kristine Bonnevie began linking morphology (study of physical shapes), inheritance, racial differences, embryological processes, and symmetry or likenesses to certain ridges and lines on the hands. The studies grew more intense and precise in the early part of the twentieth century.

As an example, it was noted by two researchers in 1940 that epileptics had bizarre fingerprint patterns, and that schizophrenics displayed abnormal finger postures. Too, these early studies began mentioning a genetic link, although not so much was known about the heritability of personality and temperament at the time.

By the mid-1940s, dermatoglyphic studies were in full swing as an accepted discipline in the medical profession, so much so, that in 1970 the *Journal of the American Medical Association* ran an editorial stating, "The human hand is a unique organ from which an extraordinary amount of clinical information may be derived." Yet, while it seems that never before has the hand been so thoroughly investigated by the scientific community, disagreement exists about its degree of usefulness.

Much of the diagnostic information uncovered by researchers leads to the fetus in the womb. They believe that telltale ridge patterns and palmar lines occur when prenatal testosterone circulates in both male and female fetuses prior to the fourteenth week of gestation. The patterns last a lifetime, changing only in their depth due to environmental factors. Anthropologist Cheryl Sorenson Jamison of Indiana University says that early theories developed in 1929 suggest that ridges develop along the paths of the underlying peripheral nerves.

One of the premiere sleuths on the trail of a link between the hand, the brain, and giftedness was the late Norman Geschwind, a neurologist at Harvard Medical School. Geschwind and his colleague, neurologist Albert Galaburda, proposed that the level of the male hormone testosterone in the developing fetus is a key factor in determining how the brain is organized. According to the Greschwind Hypothesis, cited in the *Journal of Physical Anthropology* in 1987, "The exposure of the fetus to an excess of testosterone is a causative factor implicated in the development of dyslexia, as well as in the development of such other features of neurological organization as math giftedness, left-handedness, stuttering, migraines, and immune deficiencies. This critical hormone has been found to be circulating in both male and female fetuses during the prenatal period when dermal ridges are formed."

Hormone levels can be affected by things like stress on the mother during pregnancy and chemicals from the environment. Variations in the hormone level in boys, Geschwind hypothesized, would result in a less developed left hemisphere and such brain activities as speech and handedness—normally located in the left side of the brain—would be transferred to the right side of the brain. This would lead to left-handedness, since the right side of the brain controls activity on the left side of the body. It has been found that left-handed people have a much higher incidence of dyslexia, migraines, allergies, autoimmune disorders like arthritis—and talent in math. Left-handers also may have larger corpus callosums, the area that joins the two halves of the brain, according to John Briggs, author of *Fire in the Crucible*.

Stanley Coren, psychology professor at the University of British Columbia, Vancouver, Canada, said that specific fingerprint patterns are associated with Down's syndrome, Turner's syndrome, Klinefelter's syndrome, de Lange's syndrome, Rubinstein-Taybi's syndrome, and others. In some cases, a small number of mothers of people with Down's syndrome may have abnormal dermal ridge patterns.

Today, the connection between hands and health through dermatoglyphics has been advanced because of sophisticated studies in human genetics, anthropology, neurobiology, and other sciences. Current studies hold the potential that future physicians may be able to diagnose everything from alcoholism and schizophrenia to a propensity for arthritis as the result of studying a patient's hand.

I. Newton Kugelmass, M.D., in an introduction for *Genetics of Dermal Ridges*, says that about twenty-five diseases ranging from phenylketonuria to schizophrenia can now be identified from the study of dermatoglyphics, combined with new knowledge of human chromosomes.

DERMATOGLYPHICS AND PALMISTRY

Several scientific researchers have been interviewed for this book, some of whom, although heavily involved in the study of dermatoglyphics, shun its connection to the term, "palmistry." Others, however, find the connections interesting and valuable.

Harold Cummins, author of *Fingerprints, Palms, and Soles*, writes, "In its broadest scope, dactylomancy extends to the reading of past, present, and future, as in the similar pseudo-science of palmistry. To the extent that dactylomancy concerns itself with a search for signs of constitutional makeup it merits attention as genuine scientific inquiry. As an object of investigation, this is not so far-fetched as it may seem to be at first thought. Since flexion creases and dermatoglyphics vary in other constitutional expression, a correlation between dermatoglyphics and the character-temperament constitution may be ultimately demonstrated."

During an interview with Cathy A. Stevens, M.D., a physician and researcher at University of Utah Medical Center, she said that the medical establishment has been talking seriously about palmistry since the 1800s, and she brings up the subject when she gives lectures on dermatoglyphics. In a paper that she wrote for an article in the *Journal of Pediatrics*, Stevens says, "Hand creases have been studied for thousands of years by palmists or chiromancers, but only in the last fifty years has medical science attempted to study these creases in relation to medical disorders. Recently we were involved in the case of a baby who was exposed to carbon monoxide at eighteen postmenstrual weeks of gestation. The baby had multiple congenital anomalies, and displayed absent flexion creases of the fingers." (Flexion creases are found at the wrist, the joints, and the base of the fingers, and account for the lines of Life, Head, and Heart.)

Exposure to carbon monoxide during fetal development could cause chromosomal damage, and appears to leave clues, such as altered flexion creases on the palm and an extra crease on the first joint near the tip of the fingers, according to those studying dermatoglyphics.

What Are Dermal Ridges?

We are mostly familiar with the ridges that make up the fingerprint patterns. These same type ridges, visible to the naked eye, are also found on the mounts of the palms (called volar pads by medical researchers). A more thorough discussion of these mounts is found in Chapter 10. They include the mounts found beneath the fingers, beneath the thumb (Venus in palmistry), on Luna, lying opposite Venus on the little finger side of the hand, and on the Lower Mount of Mars (lying on the arch between the thumb and the Finger of Jupiter). Traditional fingerprint patterns are also used. These ridged pads, or mounts, enabled early humans to grasp the various materials that made up their world, from tree branches, to eventual tools, without slippage.

The ridges consist of numerous sweat glands and pores, which is why the hands so easily become moist from temperature variations or emotional disturbances. Some theories indicate that dermal ridges develop along the path of underlying peripheral nerves. For example,

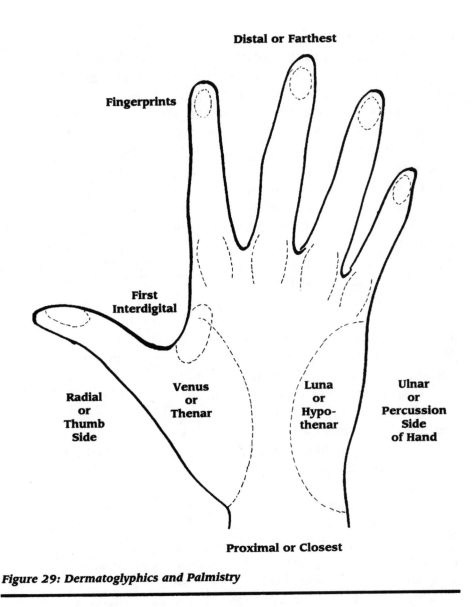

Figure 29: Dermatoglyphics and Palmistry

the peripheral nervous system is involved in numbness or tingling feelings in the hands. The ridges also consist of numerous nerve endings, adding to the sense of touch.

The accompanying graphic (figure 29) of the locations of dermal ridges includes the modern terms used in the study of dermatoglyphics, and those used by palmists.

What Causes the Ridges?

The dermal ridges are formed prior to the fourteenth week of gestation during the time an abundance of testosterone flows about the developing fetus. It can be likened to water flowing across soft ground, cutting grooves in its wake. At the same time, the nervous system is under development, and influenced by the flow. Too much or too little testosterone, as well as other assaults to the developing fetus, result in interruptions to the usual development of the ridges. Hence, telltale ridge patterns are formed. Testosterone also stimulates the production of Nerve Growth Factor (NGF), and Epidermal Growth Factor (EGF); so much is happening during this critical stage of development.

Robert J. Meier of Indiana University in Bloomington, considered one of the country's foremost authorities on anthropological dermatoglyphics, says that studies done at Harvard over the last ten years indicate that during the eighth and fourteenth weeks of prenatal development excess testosterone circulating in the fetus might delay development of the right side of the brain, which can alter an infant's autoimmune system and lead to conditions such as asthma and arthritis. Many other conditions are associated with the flow of testosterone at this critical period, including left-handedness. "The later the development, the more ridges are formed on the hand," says Meier. "So it's possible that delay of a week or so could profoundly affect development. It could make quite a difference in the number of ridges formed."

Chromosomal aberrations, that is, genetic traits, also manifest themselves on the dermal ridges. Congenital traits that can be inherited, obtained during pregnancy, or inflicted during childbirth, also show on the hands. Congenital dysplasia is one of these, affecting the bone structure of the palm and fingers.

Chromosomes are the threadlike structures in the center of a cell that carry the genetic information that controls inherited traits. Thus, dermal ridge arrangements are determined in the fetus and offer records of their growth distribution in the womb. The configurations are determined partly by hereditary and partly by accidental or environmental stress and tension in the fetus between the third and fourteenth week of gestation—a critical period for the flow of testosterone—since it affects the structures of the brain and the nervous system.

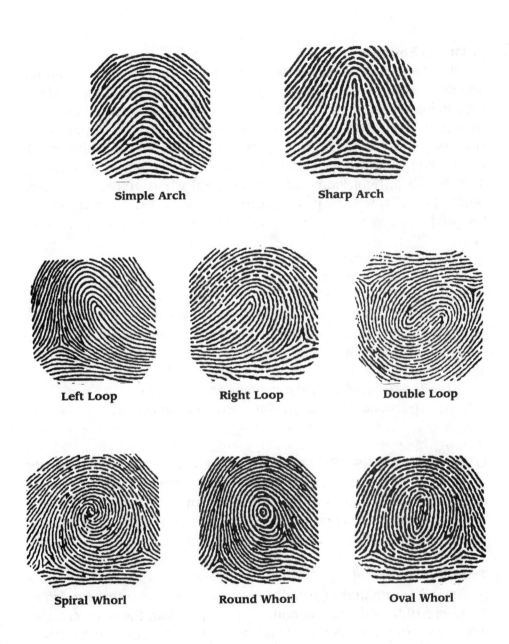

Simple Arch **Sharp Arch**

Left Loop **Right Loop** **Double Loop**

Spiral Whorl **Round Whorl** **Oval Whorl**

Figure 30: Basic Fingerprint Patterns

Patterns Emerge

In the study of dermatoglyphics, scientists have developed various methods of identifying, comparing, and measuring the dermal ridges. First and foremost in the study of dermatoglyphics is classification of the fingerprint and other dermal ridge formations. Stanley Coren of the University of British Columbia in Vancouver developed a classification of eight fingerprint prototypes much in use today: a simple arch, sharp arch, left loop, right loop, oval whorl, spiral whorl, round whorl, and double loop. These same patterns can be found on the major mounts of the hand:

○ A simple arch is a gentle, flowing arch.
○ A sharp arch is a nearly pointed arch.
○ A left loop leans toward the little finger.
○ A right loop leans toward the thumb side of the hand.
○ Double loops consist of two oval-shaped loops.
○ The oval whorl is circular-looking with an oval-shaped center.
○ The spiral whorl has a spinning appearance.
○ The round whorl is circular with a circular center.

OTHER MARKINGS USED IN THE STUDY OF DERMATOGLYPHICS

In addition to the general pattern of the dermal ridge formations, their cores and triradius also serve as information to those studying dermatoglyphics. The core or inner terminus in skin ridge formations is at the approximate center of these patterns.

Triradius

The triradii (plural of triradius) is the point where three different directions of the curved line patterns in a print join together, creating a triangle. They indicate the center point of the mount, and are found principally on the fingertips; on the two major mounts of the hand—the thenar (Venus) and the hypothenar (Luna); at three points between the fingers; at the third phalanges (the section closest to the palm) on the fingers; at the wrist; and between the thumb and the index finger (Jupiter), at the top of the mount of Venus (Lower Mars in classical palmistry). These areas are also the most visible dermal ridge formations.

Triradius   Core

Figure 31: Basic Fingerprint Patterns

Researchers, then and now, determined that the inherent ridge patterns don't change throughout life. In 1892, Sir Frances Galton, an early pioneer in the study of dermal ridges, proved this by taking prints of the same person over a period of thirty-one years. He noted, however, that trauma to the ridges, such as scaring, could create breaks, folds, or other malformations in the original patterns.

Ridge Counts

Scientists studying dermatoglyphics use the center of the triaridii as the point where they begin counting ridges, but do not include the triaridii in the count. Counts are made from one triradius to another. The angles created by the triradius, if the lines are extended by marking them, appear to be greater in females than males.

Researchers use the count, among other things, to determine inherited characteristics. It has been found that monozygotic twins (from one egg) have similar counts and that offspring have counts similar to a parent from whom they have inherited certain characteristics. The counts are frequently different on the left and right sides of the body, in keeping with biological studies that show differences in structures on the two sides of a body. Finger ridge counts, though, usually number more on the right hands, unless the person is left-handed. It has also been noted that malformations of the hands and feet are associated with abnormal ridge arrangements.

DERMATOGLYPHIC MEDICAL OBSERVATIONS

One of the most studied conditions is Down's syndrome. Since it is a genetic abnormality, it leaves traces in the hand, such as a transverse alignment (lines at right angles to the major lines) running from one side of the palm to the other. They are usually formed with a triradius near the center. The ridges themselves might appear as short, broken segments. The fingertips mostly display ulnar loop patterns (loops that bend toward the little finger side of the hand), with few whorls and arches present. (See Chapter 8 on lines.)

Another manifestation, "trisomy," which involves the chromosomes, shows itself in such abnormalities as some forms of mental retardation, cleft palate, and eye and ear deformities. Dermal ridge distortions include a large triradius high up in the hand, just beneath the fingers.

Psoriasis, a skin disorder characterized by red patches and thick, dry scales, may also be genetic. Some researchers have found that a greater frequency of whorls show on the ring finger (Saturn). Other genetic defects that have been studied through dermatoglyphics are congenital heart defects, Marfan's syndrome, and ichthyosis, an inherited skin condition in which the skin of infants is dry and cracked like fish scales. In the case of congenital heart defects, the lower triradius, usually found near the wrist, is found higher up in the palm closer to the fingers.

A predisposition to poliomyelitis (infantile paralysis) may also manifest itself on the dermal ridges. Researchers believe whorls may be increased, and arches diminished. Schizophrenia, too, has come under scrutiny, with the possibility of increased complex patterns in ridge formations in some forms of the disease. Also, the usual number of skin ridges counted from triradius to triradius is reduced in certain types of schizophrenia. Certain ridge formations may also be present in diabetes mellitus, such as a displaced lower triradius.

Sorenson-Jamison is studying the effects of dyslexia on the hand. Acquired dyslexia, which is believed to be the result of an anomaly that takes place during the fetal development of the central nervous system, differs from dyslexia caused by simple difficulty in learning to read despite average or above average intelligence, and instructional opportunities. Sorenson-Jamison found that subjects with acquired dyslexia (fetally developed) had higher frequencies of loops in certain parts of both hands, including the hypothenar area (Luna), and a misplaced triradius on the left palm. In all, the left palms of males and females showed greater dermal ridge formation differences.

Other conditions that are also acquired during the tenth to fourteenth weeks of gestation when excess testosterone is circulating, and which may show up on hand patterns, include stuttering, migraine headaches, some forms of leukemia, diabetes, auto-immune diseases such as arthritis, left-handedness, some forms of psychosis, epilepsy, and mathematical giftedness. Persons with condition that affect the hands and limbs, such as webbing (zygodactyly), also show erratic dermal patterns.

"The new studies may help establish something of the timing as it might interfere with normal childhood or early fetal development. It would say that the developing fetus should be in a proper environment. Dermatoglyphics may be indicative of a problem and eventually it could be used as a screening process; but for now, it is much too early. As it now stands, it is only being used after the fact," says Meier.

☞The left and right palms of one person are never exactly alike. The ridges on the left hand are usually finer than on the right hand of a right-handed person.

☞Women tend to have a higher frequency of arches, fewer radial loops, and usually fewer whorls than men.

☞Men have wider spaces between the ridges than women, but this may be do their larger-sized bodies.

☞Similarities in the dermal ridges are often found among relatives, and monozygotic twins (grown in one egg that splits evenly).

☞The thumb pattern is most likely to be different from the right and left hands of individuals.

☞There is evidence that the diversity of ridge counts from finger to finger is under genetic control.

☞Monkeys have similar dermal ridge patterns to humans.

☞Some studies indicate pattern differences in different races.

☞Some studies indicate that people with narrow type heads have more arch patterns than whorls, while those with a shorter, broad heads have the opposite.

☞The ridge patterns on Egyptian mummies are intact after two thousand years.

Teratogens

Teratogenic effects, too, may show up on the hands. Teratogens are a substance, agent, or process that blocks normal growth of the fetus, causing abnormalities. They act directly on the fetus, or surrounding maternal system. Some of the known teratogens include drugs, alcohol, infectious agents (such as rubella), and cytomegalovirus, a herpes-type virus.

The period of highest vulnerability to these substances is from the third through the twelfth week of gestation. In the case of cytomegalovirus, early studies, although inconclusive, indicate a tendency for increased numbers of complex patterns (whorls and double loops) on the fingertips.

USING DERMATOGLYPHICS

Some researchers see the studies as already useful. Marvin Schuster, M.D., professor of medicine and psychiatry at Johns Hopkins School of Medicine in Baltimore, says that patients with an inherited predisposition to constipation can be separated by their fingerprint patterns from those cases caused by stress or other factors. The finding could separate the two dispositions—inherited and acquired—and save needless operations. "About 7 to 13 percent of the general population has arched fingerprint patterns, and in our group of patients [suffering from chronic gastrointestinal disorders] it was seen in 54 percent. And so we felt this would be a genetic marker for these patients," says Schuster.

These particular patients had suffered from chronic gastrointestinal disorders since about the age of ten. Many of these patients were thought to have obstructions in the intestinal tract and had undergone previous surgeries, when, in fact, they didn't need it because the condition was congenital and not correctable with surgery. A cure will be possible only when the underlying inherited, congenital cause is determined, and new treatments become available, perhaps on a genetic level.

Schuster also pointed out that since up to 13 percent of the general population has arched fingerprint patterns, not all suffer chronic gastrointestinal disorders. Yet, a person who suffers from the condition might want to check his or her fingerprints to see if arched patterns are present in order to avoid needless surgery.

Meiers points out that the palm and fingerprint ridge patterns of alcoholics tend to be more pronounced. He also says researchers have also found fingerprint associations in some women with breast cancer and in infants born with the sexually transmitted disease cytomegalovirus, associated with the herpes virus.

Dr. Lee agrees that the skin of the hands and body may be shaped by genetic factors, but says that palmar and fingerprint patterns aren't yet a useful diagnostic tool. "Looking at the fingerprints isn't going to help the patient," says Lee. But other, more obvious signs on the hand can be used in diagnosis, he adds.

Dermal ridge patterns have long intrigued man and woman. An ancient Chinese method of fortune-telling involved whorls and loops on the fingertips, although nothing was known of modern day dermatoglyphics. Here is an ancient Chinese fingerprint pattern interpretation:

One whorl, poor; two whorls, rich;
Three whorls, four whorls, open a pawnshop;
Five whorls, be a go-between;
Six whorls, be a thief;
Seven whorls, meet calamities;
Eight whorls, eat chaff;
Nine whorls and one loop, no work to do—
eat till you are old.

TRADITIONAL PALMISTRY AND FINGERPRINT PATTERNS

Palmists have long used their own interpretation of fingerprint patterns. A palmist might believe that:

Simple arch patterns can be found on the hands of people who accept life's unpleasantness quietly.

Sharp arch or tented arch patterns belong to people who have a difficult time expressing themselves. Palmists believe these people hold things in and tends to allow illness and infections easy access. This is especially true if observed on the finger of Saturn.

The tented arch signifies an emotional nature, and often, insecurity.

The loop is identified by an angled center with the lines arching around it. According to palmistry, the loop pattern is found on the fingertips of sensitive, sentimental people who are open to new ideas.

The double loop pattern is found on the hands of energetic people, according to palmists. It indicates strength from the spiritual and the physical side of a person. Double loops are a mingling of two loops with one swirling up and the other down, but with the two touching.

Whorls are seen as one classification by palmists, rather than three types indicated by Coren, and they indicate a very private, stoic individual.

Composite patterns, not identified in Coren's list of eight, is a fingerprint pattern that consists of a combination of patterns. Palmists believe people with this configuration tend to be unemotional, stubborn, curious, and dogged.

The findings in the hand, always considered an important diagnostic tool by palmists, will only be enhanced with the addition of information unraveled by the scientific community. In some instances the research adds credibility to long-held beliefs harbored by those who study palmistry. In other instances, the new findings are at odds with traditional hand reading. The student of palmistry must be willing to alter his or her thinking in order to accommodate the newer materials. Through the process of intermingling the old with the new, palmistry can be seen in a new light, one that can help a person use his or her innate potential and abilities to the utmost. Many times, even a seemingly negative characteristic can be used in a positive manner. For example, an unemotional person may be able to step into a situation where emotions are hindering the completion of a project, and get the job done. Taking a new look at palmistry allows one to be more positive and objective.

VII

FINGERNAILS

Fingernails are simply another form of skin, a protein called keratin that hardens. The nail is formed by a specialized group of cells at the root, lying behind the cuticle. The base of the nail is called the matrix, and can be viewed through the lunula, or half-moon, at the base of the nail, since the skin of the nail is thinner near the lunule. The cuticle around the nail is an extension of the finger skin geared to help protect the nail matrix from infection or injury.

HEALTHY NAILS

The nail itself is dead tissue, like the hair, and can't be nourished directly by certain vitamins or minerals. It is a myth that consuming large amounts of calcium or protein will help the fingernails grow longer and heartier. Thus, ingesting gelatin doesn't help. Because pregnant women often notice a rapid increase in nail growth, it was assumed that the extra prescribed vitamins and calcium taken were the cause. Actually, though, hormone levels affect fingernail growth, so when a woman becomes pregnant her nails tend to grow faster than ever. A hyperactive thyroid gland can also trigger fast nail growth.

The best help for nails is an overall healthful diet, wearing gloves when doing work like gardening, and using rubber gloves

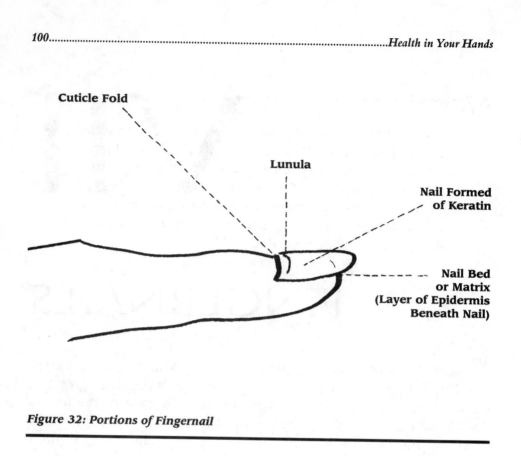

Cuticle Fold

Lunula

Nail Formed of Keratin

Nail Bed or Matrix (Layer of Epidermis Beneath Nail)

Figure 32: Portions of Fingernail

when the hands are immersed in water for long periods of time. Water penetrates nails causing them to swell, and when out from the water they dry, and shrink like leather. They chip and break more easily under these conditions. Fingernail polish remover can also dry the nails, causing them to split.

SHAPES OF FINGERNAILS

An average-length nail is usually half the length of the first phalange (or section), measured from its base to the tip of the finger. Length of the nail beyond the fingertip is not taken into consideration when determining nail length.

A typically healthy fingernail grows about one-eighth of an inch every month, thus it takes from three to six months to completely grow a new nail.

Nails grow about four times faster than toenails. Since heat increases growth, nails grow faster during the summer, especially in southern states and arid regions of the West. The nails of the dominant hand grow faster than those of the nondominant hand, and nails grow more rapidly during the day than at night.

Fingernails have four basic shapes, although many variations exist and are mentioned in this chapter. The four are: long, short, narrow, and broad.

Fingernail length is determined by growth in the first phalange on the back of the hand, and does not take into consideration that which grows beyond the fingertip.

No amount of nail care can alter the basic shape of the nails, even with false fingernails. Natural, nonpolished fingernails that shine indicate good health.

Although long nails are usually considered the ideal because of their beauty, they do not carry the strength and stamina of the individual with short nails. Too, narrow nails do not indicate the vitality of broader ones. In general, large nails indicate robustness.

CLASSICAL PALMISTRY AND NAILS

In addition to revealing insights into the health of an individual, classical palmists determined certain characteristics and personality traits through the size and shapes of fingernails.

Long nails (measured from nail bed to end of fingertip) belong to calm-tempered, easygoing individuals. They are concerned about appearance, including themselves and their surroundings. When the nails are extremely long, they might veer toward a dreamy nature, often losing contact with reality.

Short nails are found on people who tend to be curious, assertive, and full of nervous energy. Extremely short-nailed individuals can lack self-control.

Wide nails are a sign of an energetic person who is outgoing and venturesome. When short and wide, though, he or she can be overly aggressive. If the nails are long and wide, it indicates creativity.

Filbert nails, or nails that are round at the top and wide at the bottom, show a calm, peace-loving disposition. This calmness often translates to good health because the person doesn't accumulate tension and anger.

Narrow nails, when long, indicate lack of good health, coupled with nervous energy. When short and narrow, the person can be quite stubborn.

Oval nails belong to conformists. When this oval-shaped nail is extremely small, it can be an indication of poor health.

Square nails are found on the hands of orderly people.

Spatulate nails indicate insight and creativity.

Round nails, if large, indicate energy and a generous spirit. When squat, they show an envious or jealous nature.

The moon, or crescent, at the bottom of the fingernail is considered the passive, receptive, and intuitive side of a person. It engenders the feminine qualities of the universe, according to classical palmistry.

HEALTH INDICATORS OF NAILS

The following health indicators, as shown by the fingernails, include those employed by classical palmists and the scientific community.

Beau lines are horizontal ridges or indentations across the fingernail, named after Dr. Beau, a French physician who described the condition in 1846. The grooves are caused when the fingernails temporarily stop growing because of illness, according to Dr. Lee. They indicate poor circulation, diet, or other internal trauma shortly prior to their appearance, such as a serious illness, high fever, or major surgery.

Bitten nails indicate tension and worry, loneliness, or inability to solve a problem.

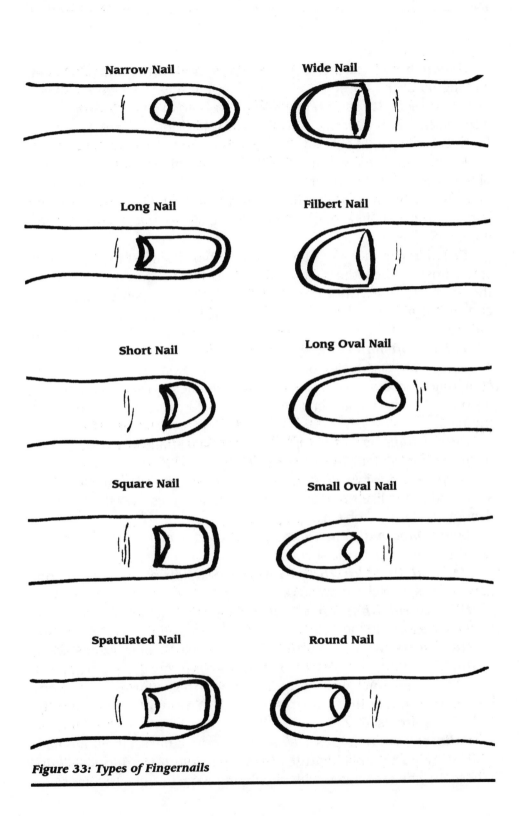

Figure 33: Types of Fingernails

Spoon nails, indicated by a concave area in the middle of nail, curving up at the tip, represent nutritional deficiencies, paralysis, and nerve disorders. Those with multiple sclerosis often have this sign. It can also indicate iron deficiency, syphilis, thyroid disorders, and rheumatic fever, according to Lee.

Raynaud's disease can also cause spoon nails. It interrupts the blood flow to the fingers in some cases, causing numbness, tingling, and often pain. It can also be linked to rheumatoid arthritis, nerve damage in the shoulders, exposure to cold, stress, drug poisoning, and protein defects.

Pitted nails indicate psoriasis. Another manifestation is linked to cirrhosis. When the nail grows out it leaves the pit because of the abnormal growth of the skin, says Lee. Pitting in orderly rows can signal alopecia areata, an autoimmune disease that results in hair loss.

Thick, soft nails, are signs of lung or congenital heart disease. Thick nails are also a sign of a condition called onychogryposis, which sometimes occurs with age. The nail becomes extremely thick and distorted. When this happens, the nails should be kept short and well-trimmed.

Curved nails, with a hump in the middle, can indicate problems in the respiratory system, colitis, or cirrhosis.

Hippocratic, or "watch glass," nails so named because they are shiny and round like the face on a watch that curves over the fingertip, denote circulatory problems.

Loose fingernails often accompany hyperthyroidism. "They grow so fast they don't stick to the skin," says Lee.

Vertical lined or fluted nails are a sign of poor digestion, nervousness, or a chronic illness.

Horizontal lines on the nails can be caused by stress, or emotional shocks to the body.

Hangnails, which take their name from an old English word "hang" for pain, consist of partly disconnected skin from the cuticle or nail fold. The hangnail should be trimmed (not torn) close with nail clippers or scissors. When infected, topical antibiotics are used.

Splinter hemorrhages may also show up beneath the fingernail, caused by particulate matter coursing through the bloodstream. "These may be associated with circulating parasites like trichinosis (a

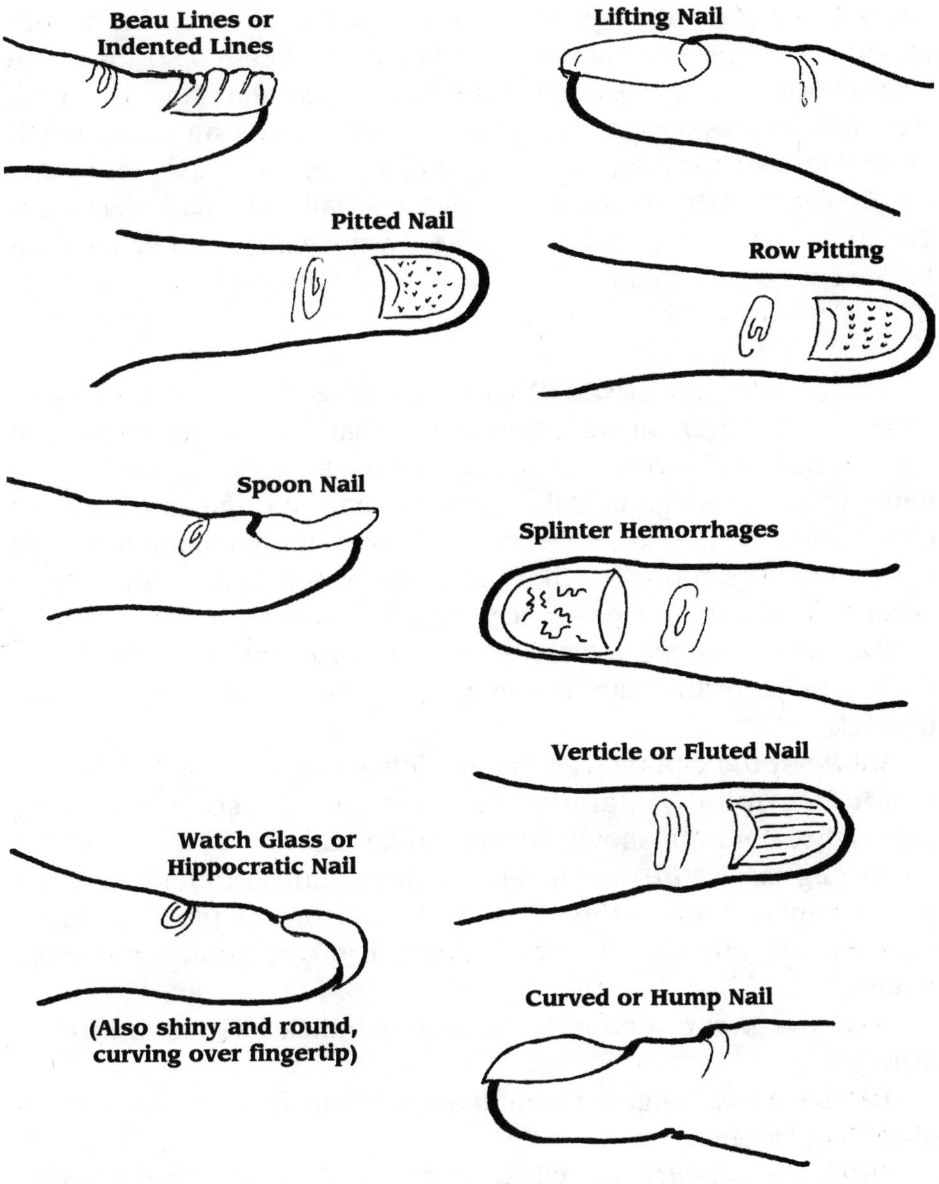

Beau Lines or Indented Lines

Lifting Nail

Pitted Nail

Row Pitting

Spoon Nail

Splinter Hemorrhages

Watch Glass or Hippocratic Nail

Verticle or Fluted Nail

(Also shiny and round, curving over fingertip)

Curved or Hump Nail

Figure 34: Types of Fingernails

parasite contracted by eating raw or undercooked pork) or with infections of the heart valve or in the blood vessels so that little clumps of bacteria or parasites are being shed and show up under the fingernail," says Lee. He recalls a patient with an unexplained fever that no one at several emergency rooms could diagnose. "The tip-off was the red streaks under her fingernails. She had trichinosis. This nice Italian lady was making her own sausage and sampling it before cooking it," said Lee.

COLOR OF THE NAILS

A healthy fingernail will appear somewhat pinkish viewed through the nail bed itself, with a somewhat shiney appearance and a well-defined moon of lighter color. A white nail bed indicates lack of compassion for life, and one too red shows and inclination toward irritability. The nail bed, like the color of the hand, can change depending upon the person's mood or health status.

Toxins or allergic reactions to medication can show up in the nails. Arsenic or thallium poisoning can create white stripes across the nail.

White spots can indicate a zinc deficiency.

Medications containing silver or gold cause grey-blue or brown discoloration showing through the nail bed.

Changes in the color of the fingernail cuticles (the thin edge of thick skin at the edge at the bottom of the fingernail) can indicate arthritis. The coloring is brought about by dilated blood vessels.

Red streaks around the cuticle may indicate lupus (a form of arthritis).

Bluish nails suggest circulation problems or metal poisoning, according to Lee.

Dark discolorations, which may spread to the finger tissue, signify malignant melanoma.

White coloration beneath the nails that are half brown or pink near the tip and the other half white, can indicate kidney failure.

White streaks down the length of the nail can result from a heart attack, kidney failure, sickle cell anemia, or treatment with cancer drugs.

👈 ───

Nails change with age. They can become more dry and brittle, and sometimes become flat or concave. The color, too, can change to yellowish or grayish tones, and does not indicate illness.

───

TRACES OF FINGERNAILS

The telltale signs of fingernails not only manifest themselves in the health of the person, but are used in identification much like the fingerprint. The ridges and valleys of the nail bed score the undercoating, creating a random array of parallel lines similar to the marks left on a bullet by a gun barrel.

Some crime lab investigators believe the fingernail striations are unique to a given nail and can offer positive identification, much like a fingerprint, according to Irving C. Stone, assistant professor of clinical pathology at the University of Texas Southwestern Medical Center at Dallas.

Stone, who is also chief of the Physical Evidence Section of the Dallas County Southwestern Institute of Forensic Sciences, has testified in Texas and other states on fingernail matches in connection with murder cases.

From the preceding information, it can be seen that nails provide direct evidence of how we treat our bodies by reflecting health or trauma. They serve as an invaluable diagnostic tool, available to both physician and layperson.

VIII

MAJOR AND SPECIAL LINES

The lines on the palm of the hand serve as guides to understanding the very nature of an individual. In classical palmistry the three major lines, Life, Heart, and Head, lay the groundwork for interpretation of all the numerous lines on the palm. No one line by itself sums up the person's characteristics. Rather, they must be considered as a unit with separate parts. Patterns emerge, such as a strong Line of Head dominating the Line of Heart. This tells the reader that the head rules the heart. Many other patterns will also manifest themselves, and through an understanding of these lines, the student of palmistry can fit the pieces together for a complete picture of an individual. This picture, once assembled, offers insight into an individual's physical, mental, and spiritual health status.

WHAT CAUSES THE LINES?

Scientists refer to the lines of the hand as "flexion creases," although some say the term is misleading since the lines are not caused by hand or joint movement. The lines or creases on the inside of the arm at the elbow joint are true flexion creases. "Palmar creases" is another widely used term.

Cathy A. Stevens, M.D., of the University of Utah Medical Center in Salt Lake City, says, "These things were being talked about in palmistry in the 1800s and I have some old drawings from India from thousands of years ago indicating certain palmar creases to tell the length of life. I show these to people when I give talks on these creases," she says. The creases are determined genetically, or from conditions in the environment when a baby is in the uterus, according to Stevens.

Some scientists who study ridge formations as clues to genetic and environmental malformations believe that as the hand is formed the skin curvature is so strongly concave and has such a sharp fold in certain places on the hands that ridges fail to form, and in its place the creases display themselves.

Others believe the major lines are actually portions of the palm that are more firmly attached to the underlying structure of the hand than elsewhere. Also, scientist Wood Jones wrote in 1920 that the major lines are marked at the site of what may be termed the skin joint, "brought into action by the movement of an underlying bony joint. But they do not always, or even generally, mark upon the skin surface the exact position of the underlying bony joint for the joint is separated from the surface by a varying thickness of intervening tissues. The point of skin movement may be translated some distance from the point of joint movement by the intervention of various tissues."

According to Stevens, though, creases can be formed where no bone or joint abnormality exists, as in the case of an extra crosswise (or transverse) crease on the fifth finger, or an extra crosswise crease on the middle finger, found on the hands of people with sickle cell disease. Whatever the cause of the creases, Stevens believes that alterations of crease patterns in the hand may serve as tools for diagnosing many congenital defects, and for showing neurologic impairment, childhood leukemia, hyperactivity, and developmental problems. Studies show, at least in some instances, that displaced folds and ridges (see Chapter 6 for more on ridge formations) are indicative of something abnormal developing in the brain, as in the case of schizophrenia, and probably are caused in those early weeks of development in the womb.

These major lines, referred to by palmists as the Lines of Life, Head, and Heart, are formed in the womb at the same time as the ridge formations are laid down, and are recognizable in twelve-week-old embryos.

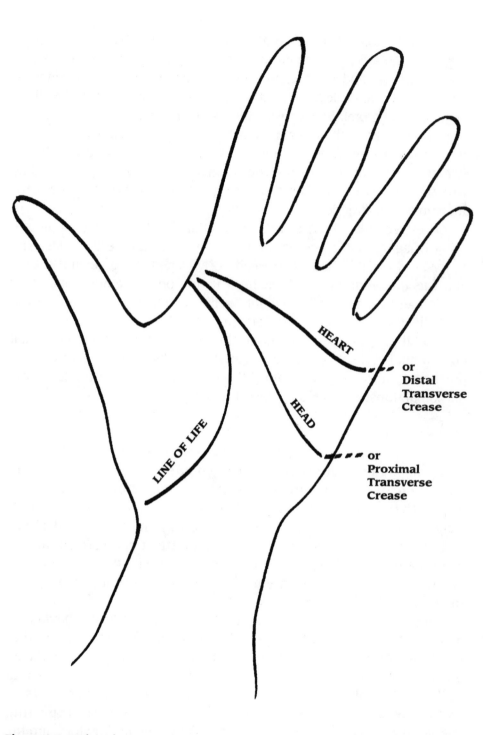

HEART

or
Distal
Transverse
Crease

HEAD

or
Proximal
Transverse
Crease

LINE OF LIFE

Figure 35: Major Lines

Sarah B. Holt, M.D., of London, author of *The Genetics of Dermal Ridges*, says that the flexion creases of the lines of Heart, Head, and Life, may be determined by the same forces that affect ridge alignment— formed during fetal development, and controlled by genes. Other lines formed in the womb include the creases at the wrist, at the base of the fingers, and at the three distinct sections usually found on the fingers between the joints. These sections are called phalanges (see Chapter 5). Scientists who study dermatoglyphics, say the major lines on the palms and fingers are not affected by age, and disappear only with decomposition after death.

Other secondary creases and grooves appear later in life, some the result of aging, and some because of changes in the person's life. The major lines of Life, Heart, and Head do not change the general course that was formed in uterus. Branches to and from these lines, and other minor lines that appear throughout the life span may seemingly alter the major lines, but the major lines remain in place.

Scientists who study dermatoglyphics call the Line of Life the "radial longitudinal crease"; the Line of Heart, the "distal transverse crease" (furthest or most distant from the wrist); and the Line of Head, the "proximal transverse crease" (closest to the wrist).

THE SIMIAN LINE

Perhaps the most widely recognized effects of genetic influence on the hand are those found on children with Down's syndrome. Researchers now acknowledge what is called the "simian line," long recognized by palm readers, whereby the upper and lower flexion creases (the lines of Head and Heart in palmistry) that run from the thumb side to the little finger side on the upper part of the palm, come together as one, usually running the entire breadth of the palm.

The print (figure 36) depicting the simian line belongs to David Fox, age twenty-eight. It was his specific request that his name be used in this book because he wants to go down in history. David is remarkable and inspirational. Following the June 28, 1992, 7.5 earthquake in Yucca Valley, California, which is only a few miles from his home, David went around his home where he lives with his mother putting everything that could break on the floor. When his mother told him the earthquake was over, he sat on the couch with his arms folded as if

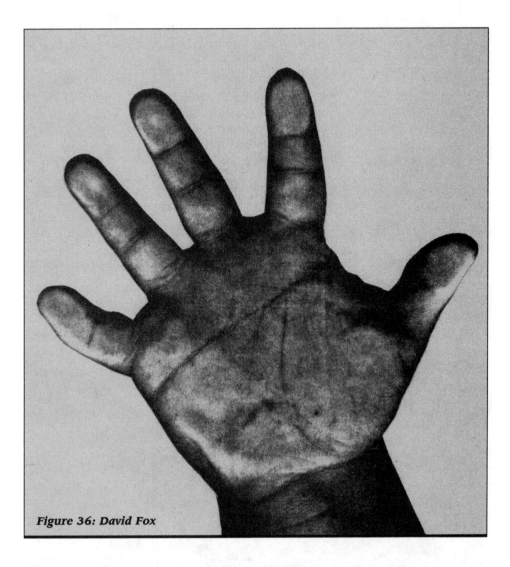

Figure 36: David Fox

waiting for another. Within two hours another major tremor hit, a 6.6, in the nearby mountain community of Big Bear, again a few miles from his home.

David speaks with authority on "Star Trek" and UFOs. He can also play the blues on his harmonica. David has a twin sister who was not affected by Down's. She is a special education instructor. Her print is shown on page 119.

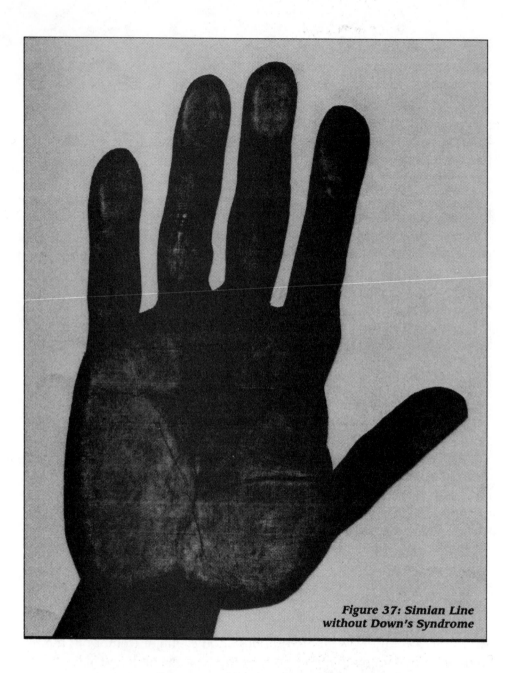

**Figure 37: Simian Line
without Down's Syndrome**

Another Type of Simian Line

Approximately 3 percent of the population who are not affected by Down's syndrome also have a simian line that runs across the breadth of the hand, according to Stanley Coren, psychology professor at the

University of British Columbia, Vancouver. The simian line can, on occasion, when it is shorter and doesn't travel across the entire breadth of the hand, indicate learning disorders, but not those associated with Down's syndrome. When this single line does not run the breadth of the hand, it is sometimes referred to as the "Sydney" line.

In classical palmistry, when the Head and Heart lines are joined, it signifies emotional intensity. With this line a person centers on one object exhaustively, be it work, love, or ideals. Although these people can be extremely loving and caring, they can also be quite unemotional if a situation is better served by using the intellect alone.

Since this line is quite rare, I was quite unnerved once at a small gathering of writers to find that three of the men present, out of about a dozen, possessed the simian line.

I next saw the simian line at a summer solstice gathering of people undergoing transformational experiences in their lives. The print depicting a simian line (figure 37) belongs to a forty-five-year-old architect, song writer, instrumentalist, and extremely sensitive man, who agreed that he has always had a problem with intensity when working on any type of project, and that it has caused problems with relationships in his life.

Ironically, the simian line is frequently accompanied by deep, irregular, ridge markings on the mounts of the palms as well as the fingers, indicating that something traumatic was occurring in the womb prior to the fourteenth week of gestation as discussed in Chapter 6. Too, not all that occurs need be negative. Math giftedness and musical ability often accompany the irregular ridge patterns.

The major lines serve as a road map to the life of an individual. And like any map, it offers choices leading to the destination. How and why these choices are made depends on a complete reading of all the lines, mounts, and particular shapes of the hands and fingers, as they work in unison to portray a complete itinerary for the journey.

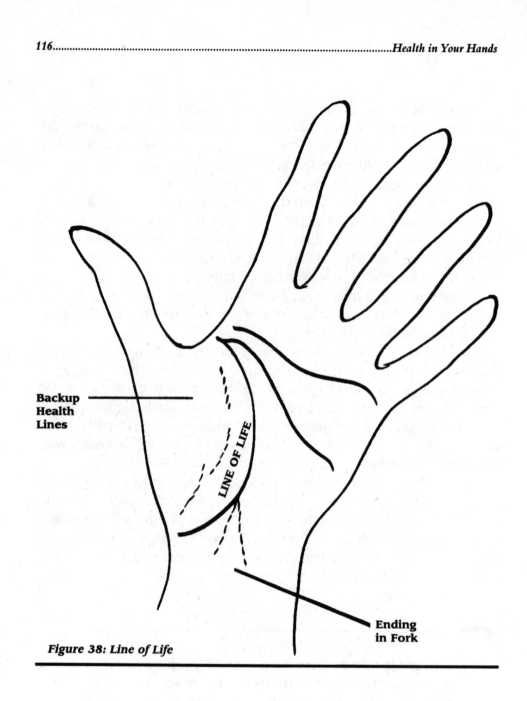

Backup Health Lines

LINE OF LIFE

Ending in Fork

Figure 38: Line of Life

THE LINE OF LIFE

The Line of Life encircles the Mount of Venus on the thumb side of the hand. It begins near the Mount of Jupiter, and usually ends near the wrist. The Line of Life does not show the length of the life. It indicates the quality and robustness of the person's life, both physically and mentally, and therefore need not be particularly long.

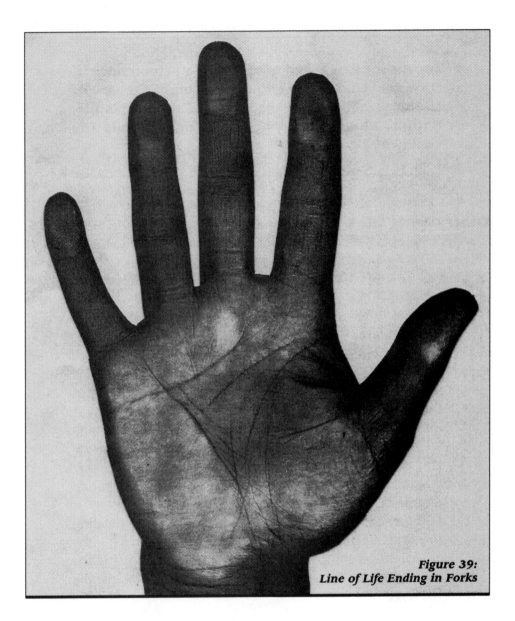

Figure 39:
Line of Life Ending in Forks

The Line of Life is often accompanied by "backup" health lines running parallel inside the line on the Mount of Venus. These backup lines often support breaks, islands, or chained formations in the Line of Life that indicate problems with health and energy. They protect the person during these unhealthful times. Note the backup health lines on the accompanying print (figure 38).

The most often asked question of a palm reader is, "Does my Line of Life show a long life?" The Line of Life does not foretell the length of a person's life. Rather, along with other markings, it tells the quality of life.

Other Line of Life Observations

The Line of Life takes many forms as it travels around the Mount of Venus and gives indications of interrupted good health, or of dissipating of energy:

○ When the line is clearly broken, with no backup line on the inside on Venus, it indicates some physical trauma at that time, but not death.

○ When chains, breaks, islands, and other marks that detract from a line are found at the beginning of the Line of Life (under Jupiter or the index finger) it indicates childhood illnesses. When the line becomes stronger further down, it shows the person outgrew the earlier childhood weaknesses. If chains or islands persist, though, it shows uneven endurance and health.

○ When the line ends in a fork near the wrist, heading toward Luna, it indicates a restless nature (figure 39).

○ If it begins fading near the end, curving inward toward the Mount of Venus, it shows gradual loss of the life force.

THE LINE OF HEART

The Line of Heart is the uppermost, deep line on the palm, lying beneath the fingers. It usually terminates on or near Jupiter or beneath Saturn. A strong, clear line indicates the person is endowed with feelings of care and nurturance toward others, including family, friends, and romantic interests.

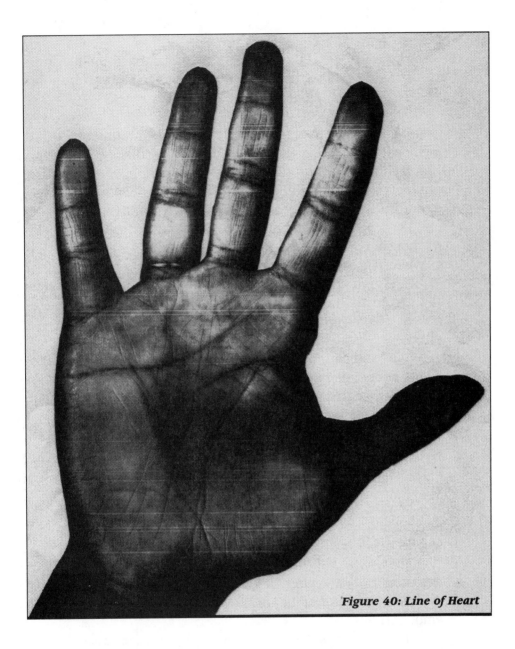

Figure 40: Line of Heart

For purposes of establishing a beginning and end to this line, which are read both ways by palmists, I read from the percussion side of the hand to its end near the Mount of Jupiter. The above print (figure 40) of a woman's hand shows a strong Line of Heart ending near Jupiter. She works in special education.

Line of Heart Notes

The Line of Heart can take several formations, each unique in its meaning, and add to the knowledge of how the person handles relationships in his or her life (figure 41):

○ Situated high on the palm, the person's intellect is involved with matters of the heart. He or she makes good, loving choices.

○ When the line is lower down, closer to the Line of Head, it shows a more cautious nature, often a sign of childhood emotional deprivation, or early traumatic relationships.

○ When the line ends beneath Jupiter (A), the person is idealistic in matters of the heart.

○ Carried to the extreme, and terminating high up nearly on the finger (B), the person can be demanding of others.

○ Ending beneath Saturn and Jupiter (C), the person is loving but not demanding.

○ If it terminates under Saturn (D), the person may be warm-natured, but not demonstrative.

○ Ending further back, beneath Apollo (E), the person is stunted in his or her affection for others.

○ A pink-toned line shows vitality in affairs of the heart, with a pale line indicating lack of vitality.

○ When the line is excessively wide and deeply colored, or overshadows the Line of Head just below it, the person lets his or her heart rule the head.

○ If it is pale and broad, the individual is aloof to emotional attachments.

○ A chained Line of Heart shows difficulties with the emotions.

○ Dark marks or spots on the line indicate a depressive nature.

○ A fork at the end of the line indicates an independent nature. The person is constantly torn between independence and forming deep bonds.

○ When the line is missing, the person can be deeply sensual, but lacking in nurturing abilities.

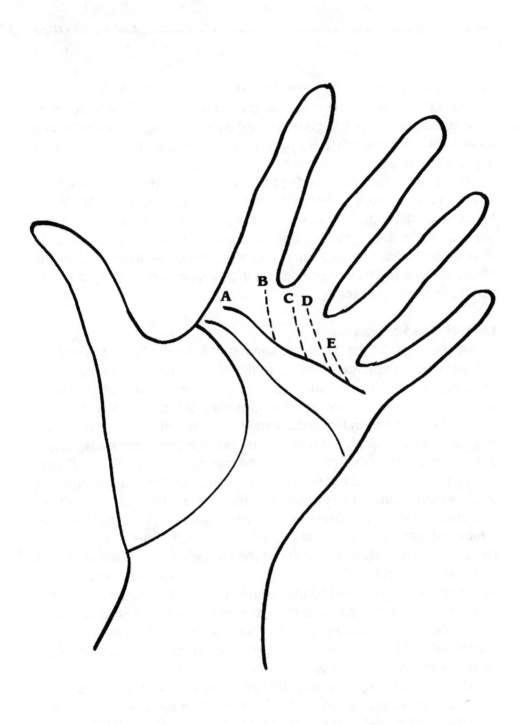

Figure 41: Line of Heart Endings

LINE OF HEAD

The Line of Head, lying below the Line of Heart in a horizontal position across the palm, generally indicates the mental interests and abilities of a person. When it appears far deeper than the Line of Heart above it, the head rules the heart.

It begins on the thumb-side of the hand, just above or touching the Line of Life (figure 42). It can head toward the fingers of Apollo or Mercury, or slope gently toward the Mount of Luna, or head in a fairly straight line to the opposite side (percussion) of the hand. A long Line of Head indicates mental acuity, and when it begins higher up on the Mount of Jupiter (D), it shows leadership ability. Too high up, though, and it indicates arrogance.

Line of Head Marks

Beginnings: When the line is separated from the Line of Life (A), it indicates an independent nature and self-confidence. If the space is extremely wide, the person is rash in judgment, and lacks caution. Touching the Line of Life at its beginnings (B), indicates a cautious nature, but if it separates immediately, the person is more open and has the ability to adapt. When it cuts through the Line of Life (C), it denotes an over-sensitive nature, and, perhaps, irritability. If it cuts through the Line of Life, and touches lower Mars (the raised puff just up from the thumb on Venus), it signifies an inquisitive nature. Sometimes the person can seem overbearing, but it is due to his or her innate curiosity. It is important to note the beginnings of the Line of Head since it reveals so much about the individual's outward approach to life and to work.

Endings: Angling toward the Mount of Luna (A), it promises a good imagination, especially if it forks at the end. Too much slope, though, creates depression. Ending near Mercury (B), it promises business and mathematical ability. Ending near Apollo (C), or cutting upwards to the mount, shows talent in the arts.

The line has only one negative position (D), and that is when it angles down toward the Line of Life and travels in the same curve, it can be a sign of suicidal tendencies. When the line ends in a fork on the percussion side of the hand, it can indicate which parent the subject is most like. On a woman's hand if the lower line of the fork is longest, she is more like her father than her mother. If the upper fork is longest, she takes after her mother.

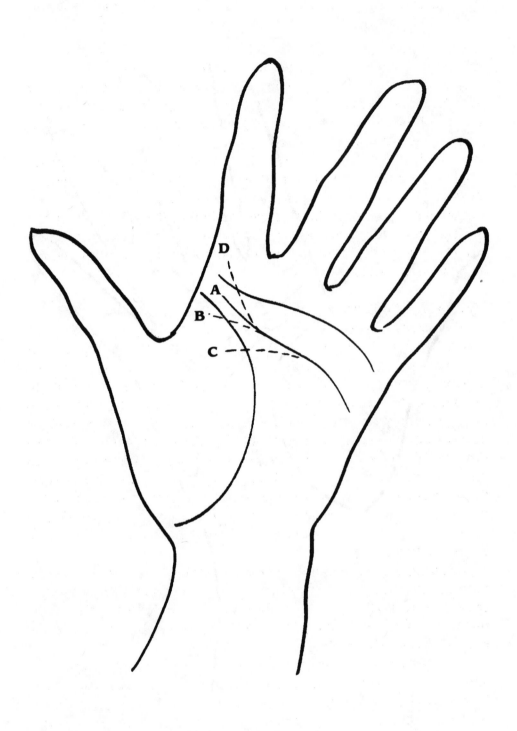

Figure 42: Line of Head Beginnings

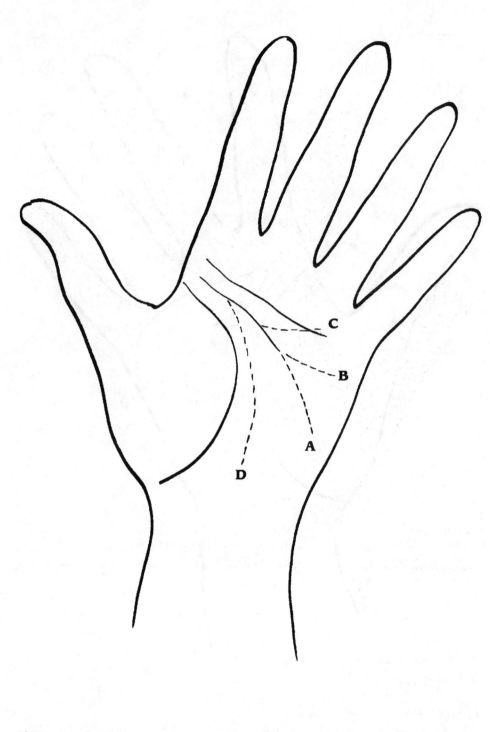

Figure 43: Line of Head Endings

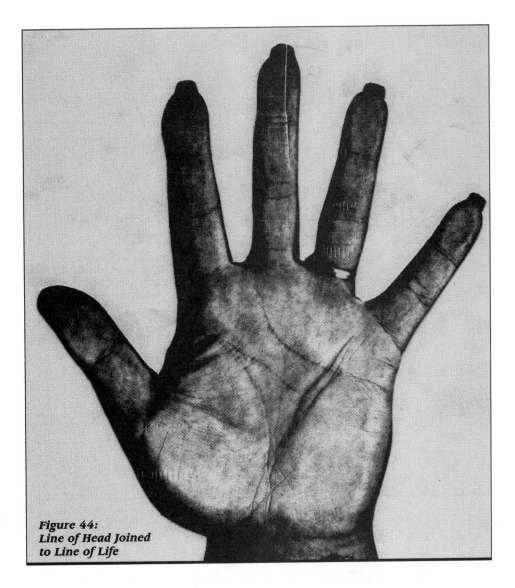

Figure 44:
Line of Head Joined
to Line of Life

On a man's hand, the opposite is true. A longer upper line indicates a likeness to the father, and a longer lower line means the man is more like his mother.

Line of Head Subtleties

Just as the beginnings and endings of the Line of Head tell something about the person's personality and temperament, so do other subtleties:

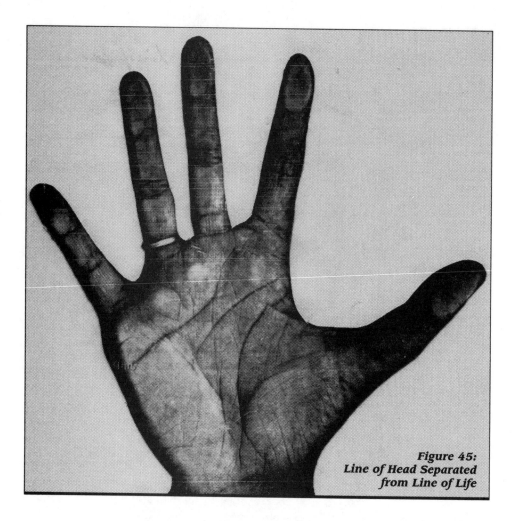

Figure 45:
Line of Head Separated
from Line of Life

○ A narrow space between the lines of Head and Heart is the sign of an introvert, while a wide space indicates the extrovert.

○ A broad Line of Head indicates an active, physical approach to life, while a thinner line denotes a mental approach.

○ A broken Line of Head means a poor memory.

○ A weak line indicates difficulty in concentration.

○ An extremely short line indicates materialism.

○ Breaks in the line show instability in the person's life

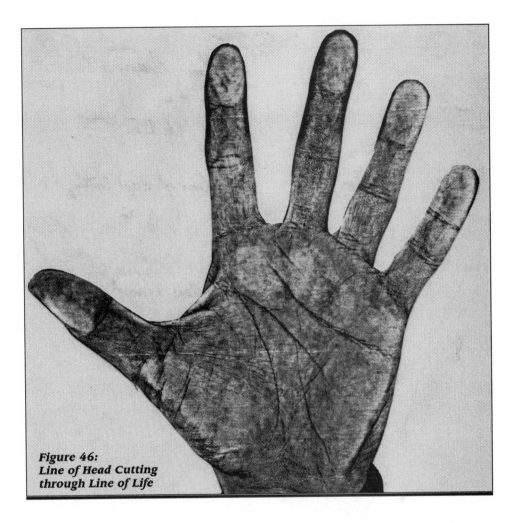

Figure 46:
Line of Head Cutting
through Line of Life

works and plans, often brought about by traumatic events
in his or her life.

○ A double Line of Head means the person is both
intellectual and intuitive.

○ If a fork at the end (on the percussion side of the hand) of the
Line of Head shoots toward Luna, it adds imagination to the
attributes of the line. If it travels too far into the Mount of Luna,
the person will be overwhelmed by his or her imagination.

○ One branch of a fork at the beginning of the line, resting
on the Mount of Jupiter, promises decision-making abilities.

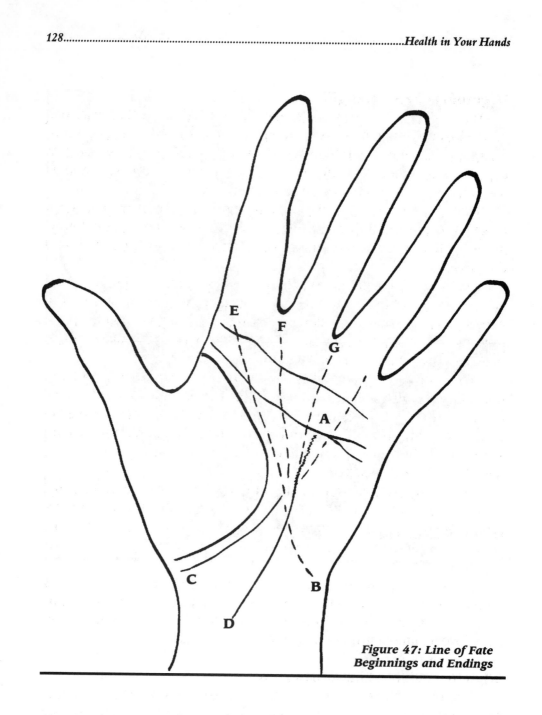

***Figure 47: Line of Fate
Beginnings and Endings***

LINE OF FATE

The Line of Fate demonstrates the career motivations of the individual. Where this line begins and ends, plus the branches that shoot off from it, tell of career changes, and offer fresh insights into the person's potential.

Beginnings and Endings

The Line of Fate usually begins near the wrist and travels toward one of the finger mounts (figure 47). Frequently, it forks in several directions. It can also begin beneath the Line of Head (A) and travel downward. In order to determine which direction it heads, the rest of the hand and its markings must be taken into consideration.

If the hand shows that the person was a late bloomer, that is, he or she sort of drifted through life until at least the thirties, the line is more likely to start at the Line of Head and travel downward toward the wrist.

The Line of Fate can also begin on the Mount of Luna (B). In such a position, the person is intuitive and can feel the pain of others. The marking can be a fortunate sign if other markings on the hand show the person to be psychologically strong. If not, the person will take on more than his or her share of others' troubles.

The Line of Fate can also rise near the wrist, springing from the Line of Life (C). In such a position, if it travels upwards close to the Line of Life the person remains tied to the parents throughout life, often interfering in the person's personal growth. More often than not, though, the Line of Fate begins at the wrist (D) and travels upwards.

The major contribution of the Line of Fate is its coping ability. When other lines indicate setbacks, such as problems with health, relationships, work, and finances, a strong Line of Fate means the person, through his or her own vitality and energy, can overcome the events.

It is one of the most changeable of the major lines, and serves as a barometer of the person's inner drive. When one lacks a Line of Fate, he or she can have a very pleasant life, but is less in control of his or her own fate than those who possess the line.

What Your Line of Fate Indicates

The direction to which this line, or branches from the main line, heads tells the reader something about the working goals of the individual, and those goals and plans might change through the years:

○ A Line of Fate ending on the Mount of Jupiter (E) shows leadership ability. When it runs into the finger itself, the life is governed by a desire for power.

O Ending on the Mount of Saturn (F), it shows success in the pursuit of an endeavor. Running into the finger itself, the person will carry things too far. It is sometimes found in this position on the hands of women who cling tightly to their children throughout their lives.

O Ending between Saturn and Apollo (F), it shows success in the technical arts.

O When the line ends on the Mount of Apollo (G), it shows an attraction to the arts. If the mount is raised, and the Line of Fate strong, the person will find career success in the arts.

O Offshoots from the Line of Fate indicate career changes, with branches heading toward Mercury signifying financial success. Toward Apollo, it means success in the arts. And toward Jupiter, success in managerial positions.

O Breaks in the line tell of temporary setbacks.

O If the Line of Fate is closely connected to that of the Line of Life, the person will be tied to his or her parents into adulthood.

O A wide space between the Line of Fate and the Line of Life indicates an early separation from the parents. Sometimes this space will appear wide at the beginning near the wrist and curve in more closely to the Line of Life as it travels up the palm. This indicates the person will become more closely aligned with the parents as he or she grows older.

All the major lines are usually clear, deep, and strong. It is part of life that people experience setbacks, disasters, emotional upsets, interferences, and that they don't always make the best decisions. But these lines clearly give evidence of the major goals, personality, and temperament of the individual, and are an invaluable tool in reading the hands.

Additionally, because these lines continue regardless of imperfections, they serve as guides to the person's development, and the knowledge that he or she will continue to grow. As well as triumphs of the past, and those waiting in the future, we are built on the debris and imperfections of the past, present, and future, and these major lines mark the way for the journey.

Some individuals have more than one Line of Fate. An independent Line of Fate, such as one beginning near the wrist and traveling straight up the hand, and another beginning on the Mount of Luna, indicate a need to please others. Offshoots springing from a single Line of Fate indicate career changes or dual careers.

IX

SMALL LINES AND OTHER MARKINGS

Many early medical researchers noted that highly strung, sensitive individuals have networks of small lines covering the hands. Many of these people tend to be worriers, and hence, more prone to illness. Yet, if the lines are strong, even an abundance of lines crisscrossing one another are signs of imaginative, energetic, and feeling people. They may be nervous types, but they transfer this nervous energy to mental activity. They lead full lives despite their worrying natures.

Lack of any fine lines, with only the major lines of Heart, Head, and Life standing out, belongs to people who take life in stride. They may have deep feelings and concerns, but they keep their feelings, dreams, ideas, and persuasions to themselves.

LINE OF HEALTH

The Line of Health begins on or near the Mount of Mercury and runs toward the lower portion of the Line of Life. Not all individuals have this line, and it is a good sign to be without it since it indicates excellent health if the rest of the hand is free of other health problems.

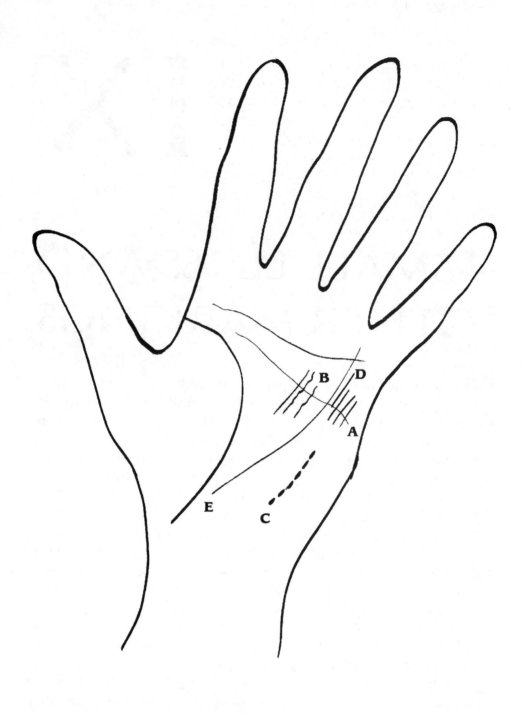

Figure 48: Lines of Health

The Line of Health need not travel diagonally all the way down the palm to give indications of health (figure 48). When formed by a number of thin lines situated close together it signifies bad digestion (A). If the line or lines are wavy, it indicates liver or gall bladder problems (B). If the line, or lines are chained (C), and the fingernails are almond shaped, the lungs are vulnerable.

A Line of Health that starts and stops between the lines of Head and Heart (D), and if accompanied by an island on the Line of Head, indicates mental blockages. If the line travels all the way down the hand and touches or cuts the Line of Life, it shows the approximate year in which the person is most likely to suffer ill health (E).

Hypertension

If the Line of Health is deep and red it signifies circulatory problems such as hypertension (high blood pressure). When found on both hands, it indicates the problem might be hereditary, which is quite possible since medical professionals now know that certain forms of hypertension run in families, as do high cholesterol counts in some people. High cholesterol can be linked to hypertension.

It's estimated that up to 33 percent of the adult population suffer from hypertension, often called the "silent killer" because it often lacks symptoms until it results in a stroke or heart attack. The only way to really discern blood pressure, is to have it taken frequently, allowing for the fact that it can vary depending on the mental or physical state of the person.

In the case of hereditary hypertension, the latest research indicates that medication is the only way to control it. Eliminating salt and fats from the diet may help, but it won't alter it much. Losing weight, though, seems to help. The American Heart Association considers the "systolic pressure" (when blood is expelled from the heart), high if it reads over 140, and the diastolic pressure (the heart at rest), above 90.

Hypertension also manifests itself in high cholesterol readings, and abnormalities in glucose and insulin metabolism. A physician should always be consulted if hypertension, or any of the following conditions are suspected.

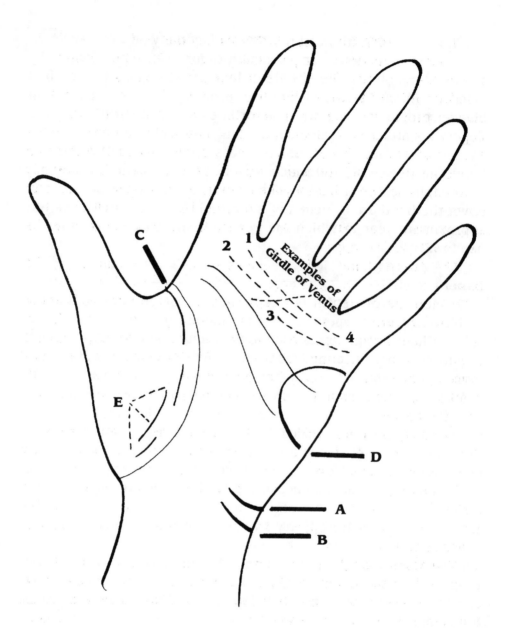

Figure 49: Girdle of Venus

OTHER LINES WITH HEALTH SIGNS

Other lines appear on the palm that provide added information about health. Not all of these lines, however, appear on all hands.

The Girdle of Venus is a fine line appearing above the Line of Heart and running toward the percussion side of the hand. Although it can begin anywhere near the Mount of Jupiter, even cutting through other lines, it usually terminates between Mercury and Apollo. It portends a love of luxury, sensitivity, and sensuality. Its owners can be unusually perceptive and bright, but they are often quite emotional and prone to hypochondria if the line is wavy, contains islands, or is chained. See graphic (figure 49), with 1, 2, 3, and 4 marked as examples of how the individual lines can appear.

The Allergy Line (A) is a small horizontal line running along the base of the Mount of Luna near the wrist. People with this marking suffer more than most from pollens, chemicals, and airborne pollutants.

The Indulgence Line (B) is frequently confused with the Allergy Line, since it, too, lies near the base of the Mount of Luna. It slants upwards, though, from the wrist bracelets, rather than running horizontal. It indicates a person who overindulges in food, alcohol, or drugs. Islands on this small line exacerbate the need for the indulgences.

Antibody or Mars Line (C) is sometimes called an attendant line. It lies inside the top of the Line of Life, running close to it. It promises extra energy, and the ability to recover fast from illnesses.

It is a major "backup" line, a type of line that runs parallel and inside the Line of Life that serves as protection in areas where the Line of Life breaks, or shows other weaknesses, such as a chained formation.

The Moon Line (D) is found on the percussion side of the hand, and rests between the Mounts of Luna and Mercury, curving into the palm. Sometimes called the "Line of Intuition," it is often found on both hands. If it is missing on the right hand, but found on the left, then the person hasn't used his or her inherited intuitive capabilities. If found only on the right hand, the person has worked hard to acquire those abilities. The opposite is true if the person is left-handed.

Backup lines (E) are fine lines found parallel to the major lines. They add strength at the time any breaks, islands, or other negative markings appear on the major line. These lines frequently appear running parallel and inside the Line of Life.

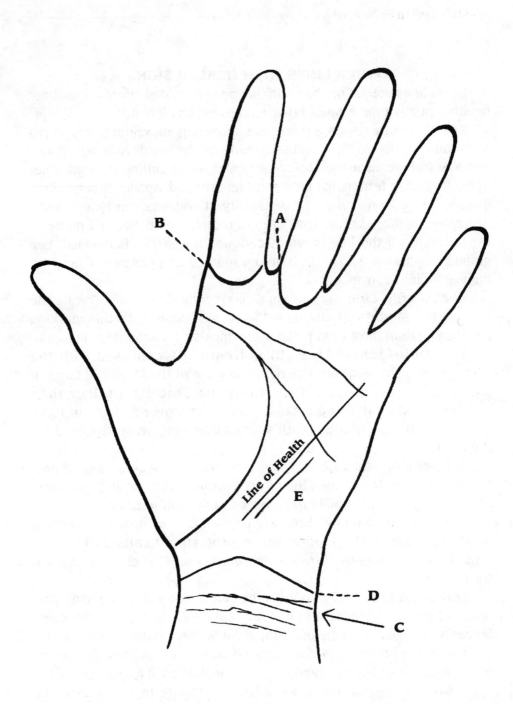

Figure 50: Rings, Bracelets, and Cephalic Lines

The Ring of Saturn (A) is a small line found at the bottom of the finger of Saturn on the palm, arching between Jupiter and Apollo. It denotes loss of energy and a tendency toward melancholia.

The Ring of Solomon (B), a small line found at the bottom of the finger of Jupiter, belongs to metaphysical adepts. Their abilities are inherent, rather than learned.

Bracelets (C) are also known as rascettes, or wrist bracelets. If found arching into the palm (D), they indicate problems with childbirth in women. If the first line is clear and unbroken, it portends excellent health. Islands or chains indicate anxiety. In classical palmistry, three strong, unbroken lines at the wrist promise long life.

The Cephalic Line running next to the Line of Health (E), on the percussion side of the hand, but shorter than the Line of Health, promises good health, and the enjoyment of sex. Another name given this line in classical palmistry is the Via Lasciva.

Small light spots on the hands can indicate temporary illness, while small dark spots mean emotional illness or upsets. Red spots can indicate fever, infections, or allergic reactions. The spots temporarily block energy on the lines in which they are found. Thus, on the Line of Heart, they are interruptions in the love life; on the Line of Head, mood swings; on the Line of Fate, interruptions in the career.

Spots are not to be confused with tiny circles that are not solid. Although circles mean much the same thing when found on the lines, if they are on the mounts of the hand, they denote added power and insight. For example, on the Mount of Jupiter, they add leadership capabilities.

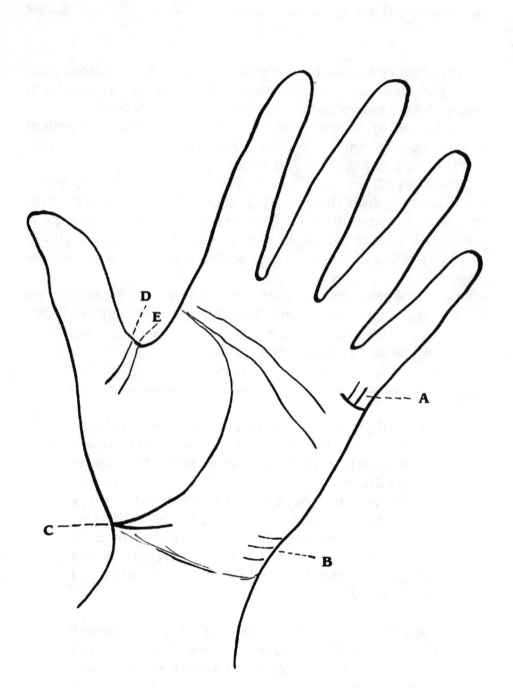

Figure 51: Children, Backup, Escape, Stubbornness, and Temper Lines

Children lines are found running vertically on the lines of marriage (A) below the little finger on the side of the palm. Deep heavy lines indicate a healthy child. The lines of children are usually difficult to see on the marriage lines and may require a magnifying glass.

Backup lines are sometimes present on the percussion side of the hand, running horizontally, just above the side of the wrist (B).

The Escape or Avoidance Line (C) is a horizontal line appearing at the bottom of the Line of Life, but not necessarily touching it. It belongs to the person who tries to escape from life and responsibilities by engaging in excesses such as drugs, alcohol, sex, or overeating.

The Line of Stubbornness (D) is located on the thumb near the bottom of the second joint (the one closest to Venus). It indicates a stubborn and tenacious nature.

The Temper Line (E) is found slightly below the Line of Stubbornness on the thumb directly above the second joint. It indicates a stubborn nature, and one given to tantrums if the person doesn't get his or her way.

☞ ————————————————————————

More men than women have hair on the back of the hands and the portion below the knuckle. It signifies a very robust nature, and one that recovers quickly from illness. If the hair is extremely plentiful, it indicates an easily aroused temper. On a woman's hands, the hair is usually finer and indicates an extremely robust nature. Lack of hair on a man's hands can indicate timidity and an inferiority complex. Although hair on a woman's hands is often viewed as "not lovely," that perception probably will change much the same way as the idea of muscular women has, which, today, is perceived as healthy and vital.

————————————————————————

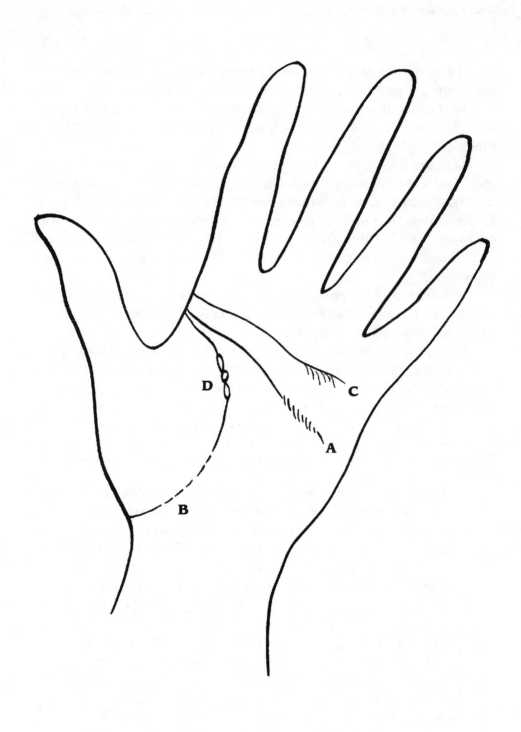

Figure 52: Lines That Sap Strength

Frayed lines (A) within major lines show loss of energy during the time they mark the hand.

Breaks in lines (B) indicate weakness at the time they appear, especially on the Line of Life. Parallel lines or squares surrounding the break add protection.

Capillary lines (C) are faint lines that droop from another line and sap energy at the time of their appearance. These lines usually fade when the trauma or illness is past.

Chained formations (D) on lines interrupt the healthy flow of that line.

The most pronounced, short horizontal lines on the percussion side of the hand lying between the bottom of the little finger and the Line of Heart once stood for lines of marriage, but can now mean lasting, or long-term relationships between the opposite sex, or same sex liaisons. Although a person may have had many love relationships throughout his or her life, only those that are still deeply imbedded in memory, or played a significant part in the person's life, will show themselves in this position.

OTHER MARKINGS

Several other markings that do not fall into the category of lines appear on the palm. They can appear independently, or on major and minor lines.

Circles (A) have the same meaning as islands, a weakness, unless they are on the mounts of the hands where they are considered a fortunate sign in connection with the qualities of that particular mount.

Cross bars (B) denote temporary restriction in the energy of a major line. Located on the mounts, it can be a hindrance. On the Mount of Venus, though, it indicates energy.

Crosses (C) on a line indicate difficulties pertaining to the meaning of that particular line.

Ladders (D) are small bunches of lines that cross a main line. They sap the energy of that line while they appear.

Spots (E) are tiny markings found on lines or mounts that bespeak temporary difficulties, sometimes associated with health. On the Line of Life, it blocks energy and indicates an illness. Found on the Line of Head, it sometimes indicates depression.

Islands (F) encroach on the energy of a line. On the lines of Fate or Heart, it means poor health for the time they appear. On the Line of Health, it means a severe illness. I have noted them frequently on women's hands on the upper portion on the Line of Life. It means problems with the reproductive organs.

The square (G), surrounding a break in a line, an island, circle, spot, ladder, or any other energy sapping mark, is a preservation from the negative effects of those markings. The square is saying, "This will occur, but it won't be permanent."

Although the cross usually signifies a temporary restriction or hindrance, that is not the case when it appears centrally located between the Head and Heart lines. In this instance, the portion of the cross making up the vertical line is part of the Line of Fate, and the horizontal line crosses it. Known as the Mystic Cross, some palm readers believe it indicates elevated metaphysical and psychic abilities.

SPECIAL MARKINGS

Special markings are those formations that appear independently of other lines. They add important character traits to the individual on whose palm they emerge.

These special markings, healer's marks, St. Andres's Cross, and friendship lines, all pertain to individuals who are people oriented. They

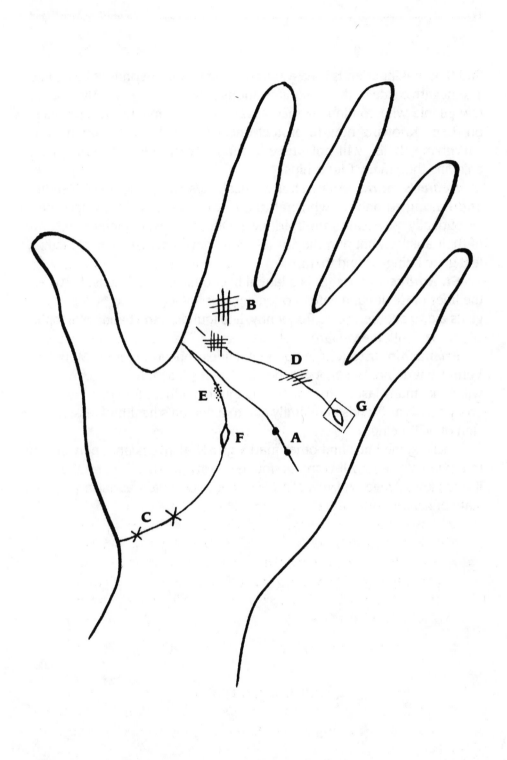

Figure 53: Other Markings

find that making friends is easy, which is generally a wonderful attribute. The negative side to these manifestations is that they frequently attract a few people who continually take advantage by dumping their problems on them. Knowing how to protect oneself from an overabundance of caregiving duties will not prevent people with these markings from enjoying their many friendships.

Healer's marks (A) are short vertical lines on the Mount of Mercury, and belong to people who naturally have an ability to help others emotionally, physically, and spiritually. Often, these people are unaware of their abilities, but find they have many friends because people simply feel good being around them.

St. Andres's Cross (B) is a lateral line found near the wrist between the lines of Health and Fate. It often denotes someone who "saves" or gives aid to another. More frequently, it is found on the hands of people concerned with the welfare of others.

Friendship lines (C) are horizontal lines appearing on the Mount of Venus that do not touch or cut the Line of Life. It signifies someone who will make many lasting friends throughout his or her life. Since support groups such as friends and family add to a person's healthfulness, it is a sign of well-being.

These small lines and other markings add richness and individuality to a person's hand. All won't be found on one palm, but when they are, it adds knowledge and reveals additional information about a person's state of health.

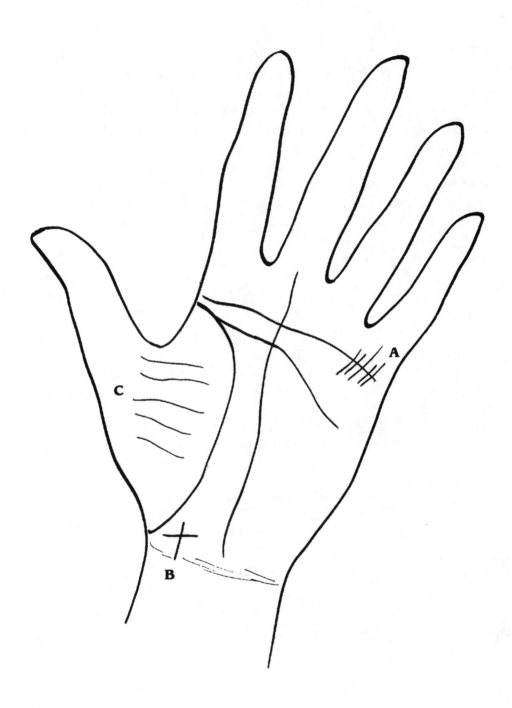

Figure 54: Special Markings

X

HAND MOUNTS

Mounts are those raised portions on the palm side of the hand found beneath the fingers, on the percussion side of the hand beneath the Finger of Mercury and running down to the wrist, and on the thumb side of the hand surrounding the thumb. Small mounts are also found on the phalanges of the fingers. Each finger has three phalanges, separated by the joints. In classical palmistry, these mounts are named after the twelve astrological signs.

Mounts are considered sources of energy, and take on specific characteristics linked to their locations. Certain signs on these mounts, such as bars, grills, cross bars, islands, and spots take away energy. Other signs, such as stars, circles, and squares, add energy. Well-developed mounts on the palm generally add stamina to a person's constitution since he or she shows active energy within the mind and body. Those with well-developed mounts tend to suffer fewer common ailments, perhaps because their minds are constantly more active and they don't dwell on minor inconveniences. They also tend to recover from illnesses more speedily than those with hollow-looking palms.

Few people have all the mounts developed, particularly beneath the fingers. Rather, the ones that show the person's particular interests and capabilities will be more prominently displayed. The mounts, especially those of Venus and Luna, should be firm and elastic to the touch. Both give important clues to the health and recuperating powers of a person. Mounts are usually more in evidence on conic and philosophic hands (water and air), than on square and spatulate (earth and fire). So when large mounts are found on the latter two type hands, they are more significant and powerful. (See Chapter 4 for the shapes of hands.)

The firmness and elevation of a mount can change with the person's mood. When a person is feeling energetic and happy, the mounts are more likely to be at their best. Check your own mounts when you're feeling great, and compare them to the times you're feeling under the weather. A noticeable difference exists.

Excessively soft or flabby mounts indicate self-indulgence. Hard mounts belong on the hands of less enthusiastic people than those with full, elastic mounts. The person with a thin hand, hollow in the center and lacking mounts, is inclined to turn his or her life over to others. The person tends to be peace-loving, idealistic, and trusting. Sometimes this can work to his or her benefit, while other times it lessens individual control over his or her life.

When the mounts are well developed and a small space in the very center of the palm is thin, it indicates an extremely sensitive person, but one who has a good grasp on life. The mounts on the palms frequently contain ridge formations similar to the person's fingerprint patterns.

EARTH MOUNT

The Earth Mount is the one mount found on the outside, or knuckle side, of the hand, and can provide one of the first clues to a person's health. It is found by holding the thumb straight pressed next to the finger of Jupiter (index finger) and observing the puff that is formed on the back of the hand next to the bottom of the thumb beneath Jupiter. When it is firm and puffy, it indicates good health and energy, and the power to recuperate from illnesses. When it is flat or soft it portends lack of energy and difficulty recovering from illnesses. People who like to be alone most of the time, usually have small Earth Mounts, and a medium sized mount indicates a person who is warm by nature, but who also enjoys his or her privacy.

Acupressure Point

The Earth Mount also serves as a pressure, or power point. Dig in with the opposite thumb and rub in circular motion beneath the padded area. As well as serving as a stimulus, it helps relieve headaches and tension.

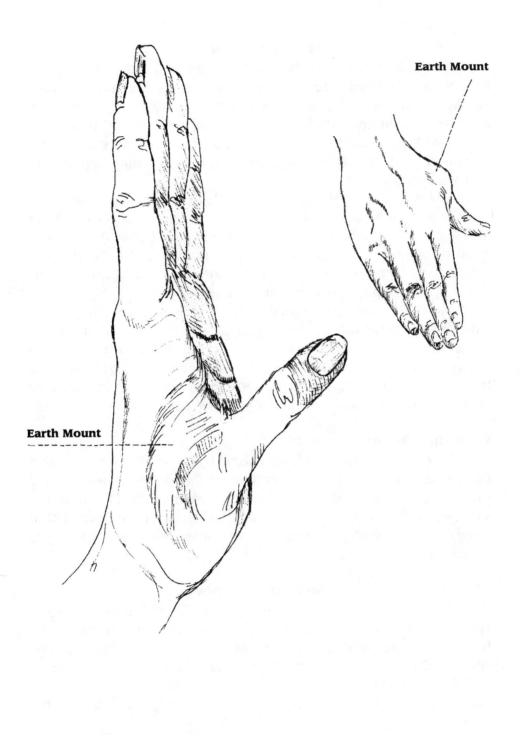

Earth Mount

Earth Mount

Figure 55: Earth Mounts

MOUNT OF VENUS

The Mount of Venus lies below the thumb and is encircled by the Line of Life. Usually puffier than any other part of the palm, it should be slightly firm and elastic to the touch. When well represented, it indicates an inner attitude of vitality and robustness. It is often linked with sensuality, but is more indicative of energy. When a person is ill, a normally healthy Mount of Venus may appear less firm than normal.

An excessively developed Mount of Venus, especially if it is soft, signifies a self-indulgent nature. The individual can be quite sensual, but also selfish. If the puffiest portion lies closest to the thumb, the person is ruled by emotions. Lower down, toward the wrist, it indicates self-indulgence. The person won't recover rapidly from illnesses because he or she likes to be pampered and catered to.

A narrow mount, determined by its border line, the Line of Life, indicates a cautious nature. The Line of Life usually comes to nearly the middle of the palm at its widest point. If still full and firm, though narrower, the person may enjoy robust health, but lack passion. Horizontal lines running across this mount, but not cutting into the Line of Life, add stamina and strength to the person's constitution.

Palm-Chin Reflex

Palm-chin reflex is a condition caused by an abnormal nerve effect that causes some people to scratch the palm in the Venus area. At the same time, the muscles of the chin and corner of the mouth on the same side of the body contract. Usually it is a minor condition, but in some cases it involves a nervous system disease and can lead to a type of face paralysis.

MOUNT OF LUNA

The Mount of Luna, sometimes referred to as the Mount of the Moon, is located on the percussion side of the hand between the Line of Heart (sometimes further down and below the Line of Head), ending near the wrist. It is associated with spirituality, imagination, occultism, and a visionary sense. This mount lies in the lower outer portion or zone of the hand which represents the inner way we deal with the outer world.

A well-developed mount often signifies creative abilities in the arts when other markings on the hand indicate an artistic bent.

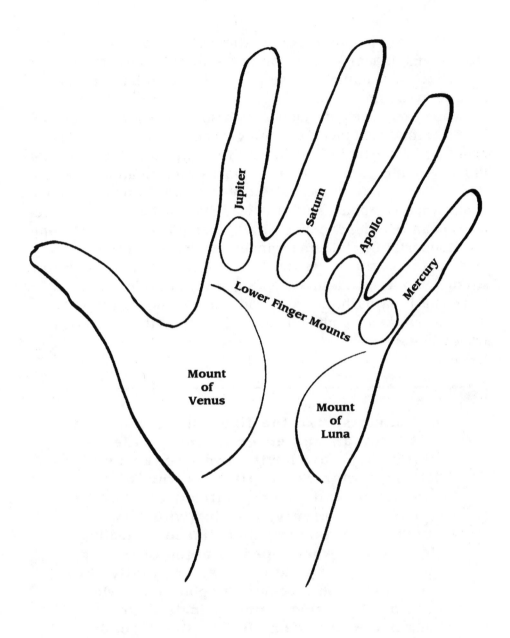

Jupiter

Saturn

Apollo

Mercury

Lower Finger Mounts

Mount
of
Venus

Mount
of
Luna

Figure 56: Major Mounts

Even though a person lacks artistic abilities, a well-developed Mount of Luna gives him or her a love of beauty, and an appreciation of nature. These people can also harbor leanings toward mysticism.

When excessively developed, and soft, it indicates obsession with the good qualities it can bring, such as spirituality, concern for others, imagination, and love of beauty. Sometimes, mental degeneration occurs due to an overactive imagination. The term "lunacy" derives from the name of the mount. A puffy Mount of Luna, when combined with a deeply marked Line of Heart, can also mean overdependence on another person. These people tend to look toward others for inner happiness and health.

A small square, triangle, or circle on this mount strengthens its good qualities. So, a well-developed Mount of Luna can be a harbinger of good and bad depending on how well it is marked, combined with other strengths and weakness shown in the hand.

The mounts, like the fingers, were named after Roman named gods and goddesses which originated with the Greeks under different names. Jupiter is the god of knowledge and power; Saturn, the god of fertility and plenty; Apollo (who kept his Greek name), was originally linked to healing; Mercury was worshipped as a god of trading, luck, and profit; and Mars, originally the agricultural god, became the god of war when the Romans turned from agriculture to war. Luna is the Latin name for the Greek goddess Selene (also called Phoebe), who eventually came to be associated with the moon. Venus (or Aphrodite) has been portrayed both as soft, sweet, and weak, but also deadly and destructive in dealing with men.

LOWER FINGER MOUNTS

Each finger is also represented by a mount lying beneath the finger on the palm, and sometimes between two fingers. It takes on the characteristic of that finger, or when lying between two of them, blends the two qualities of the fingers represented. A lack of these mounts, or of Luna and Venus, indicates lack of energy, and difficulty accomplishing goals. Usually air, water (the more pointed hands), and sometimes fire (spatulate) tend to have more well-developed mounts than the earth or square hand. Exceptions exist, though. The most well-developed mounts I ever encountered were found on a woman with square hands. She is multiply talented, a hard worker, and full of excess energy.

The Mount of Mercury

The Mount of Mercury is found just below the little finger. It gives its owner speaking ability, intuition, good business sense, an ability to rebound from emotional hurts, and medical skill. If the mount is missing altogether, so is a sense of humor.

If it is puffiest close to the side of the hand, it shows an ability to take immediate action when confronted with difficulties. If the puff rests near the Line of Heart, the person is quick in emergencies.

The Mount of Apollo

The Mount of Apollo lies beneath the Finger of Apollo. When well-developed, it shows a desire for fame and continued growth and education. It also indicates love of the arts. When excessively large, though, it indicates arrogance and vanity. Flat, and the person lacks spiritual energy. A hard lump on this mount on the left hand can indicate that the person has suffered a heart attack.

The Mount of Saturn

The Mount of Saturn lies at the base of the middle finger. When well developed, it shows a love of solitude, and a desire to improve the intellect. When excessive, especially combined with a large Finger of Saturn, the person tends toward depression and morbidness.

The Mount of Jupiter

The Mount of Jupiter lies at the base of the index finger. Like the finger itself, it denotes power and ambition. When well developed, and on a hand with other good markings, it gives the ability to manage others, leadership ability, and sometimes a desire to become involved in worthy causes.

When excessively developed, especially if the finger is exceptionally long, the person will carry the good qualities of the mount to extreme by being bossy and always wanting his or her own way.

Mounts can swell or decrease depending on the energy being exerted at the present time in the area they represent. When firm and plump, the energy is focused. When flabby, they are full of inactivity. Also, a diet heavy in sweets and carbohydrates drain them of energy and elasticity.

OTHER MINOR MOUNTS

Although the minor mounts are not as noticeable as the six major ones, and are often overlooked, they provide additional insight into the health potential of an individual since many of them give indications of energy and stamina.

The Lower Mars Mount

The Lower Mars Mount is located inside the Line of Life, and within the arch made by the thumb. A fleshy pad in this position endows its owner with the ability to withstand a great deal of physical pain. If the area is flat, it indicates an inability to tolerate much physical pain.

The ability to withstand physical pain, not only has a psychological connection, but can be inherent as well. It might depend on how the person's nervous system is wired. Too, some people have more difficulty dealing with physical pain because their childhoods were spent with families who taught them to "stuff it." Therefore, when they feel pain, they believe it is abnormal, when in reality, physical pain is a natural part of life.

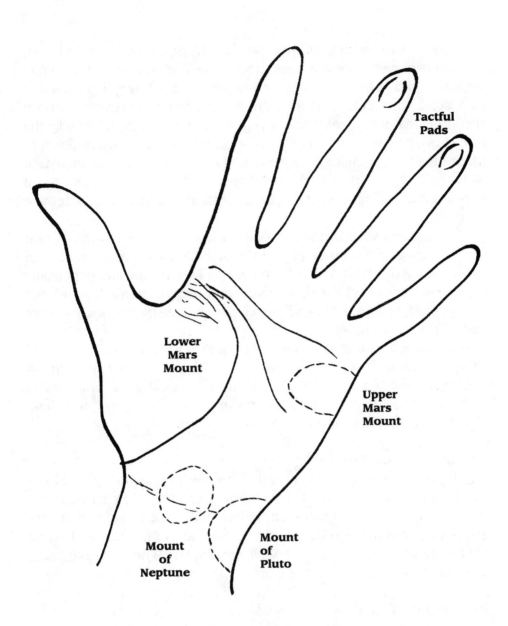

Tactful Pads

Lower Mars Mount

Upper Mars Mount

Mount of Neptune

Mount of Pluto

Figure 57: Minor Mounts

If pain is perceived as unnatural, suffering can be intensified, according to medical researchers. When attention centers on the pain, a person is "juicing up" the pain pathway. The pain pathway is first alerted by a series of electrochemical nerve impulses that release certain chemicals that sensitize nerve endings to heighten pain. Eventually the pain message enters the spinal cord where it travels up nerve fibers to the brain. Fright or anger is triggered and the body reacts with increased blood pressure, heart rate, and respiration, followed by a psychological response such as anxiety, anger, or depression—all of which exacerbate the pain.

So the ability to withstand pain is not a simple matter of one person being mentally or physically stronger than another. It can depend on early childhood experiences, be biologically and genetically determined, or reflect the person's current state of mind. If I find that the Upper Mars sign is not well developed, it cues me to look for other mitigating circumstances.

I've often found that people who can't withstand much physical pain, nonetheless, are good at dealing with psychological trauma—their own, and that of others. They can withstand great amounts of turmoil in their lives without giving up or in. And they often help others through problems.

The Upper Mars Mount

The Upper Mars Mount is found on the percussion side of the hand (the little finger side), just below the Line of Heart near the Mount of Luna. It designates an active resistance to such obstacles as illness, and an assertive nature. An individual can withstand hardships when this mount is well developed. When undeveloped, the person lacks assertiveness.

The Mount of Neptune

The Mount of Neptune is found just above the wrist bracelets on the palm side of the hand between Venus and Luna. It promises vitality, and when it joins with the two mounts it lies between, it blends the mounts' characteristics. Thus, the person would be endowed with great imaginative powers, passion, and endurance.

Tactful Pads

Tactful pads, or sensitivity pads, are found on the tip or first phalange of the fingers on the hands of some people. The pads indicate those who are sensitive to the feelings of others, and who will go out of their way to avoid hurting other people. In itself, the pad can be a good trait since it gives diplomacy to many successful administrators and leaders. Carried to extremes, though, the person can seem to be indecisive.

Also called "sensitivity pads," some palmists believe they are also found on people with highly developed senses of touch. I have noted these pads on the fingers of people from all walks of life, from carpenters to scholars, and equally distributed between men and women.

The Mount of Pluto

The Mount of Pluto is found on the palm at the lower, outer edge of the Mount of Luna. It can be quite large, and when well developed, stands for wisdom. The person with this formation is often called upon to serve as a mentor, or someone who offers sound advice to those who seek it.

Other areas of puffiness, not considered mounts, can be found on the hands around the lines. Some of these puffs indicate unsettled matters often dealing with emotional pain, or unresolved conflicts. Around the Line of Heart, puffiness can indicate a period of heartache that the person hasn't yet recovered from. On the lines of marriage, it can mean trouble within the marriage, or if a divorce or separation has taken place, the person is still grieving over the matter. Such pain and grief saps energy, and sets the stage for illness since it lowers the immune system. So it becomes important to deal openly with these matters.

Old Soul Mount

An Old Soul Mount is associated with the Mount of Pluto, since it encompasses that same area, but is much larger and spreads down

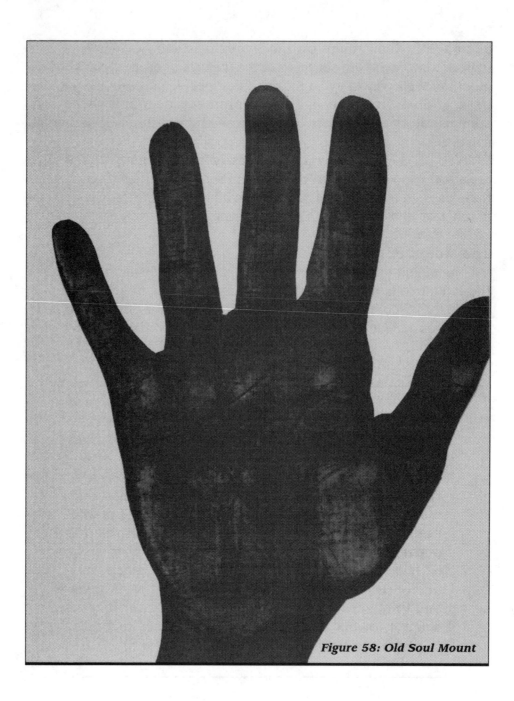

Figure 58: Old Soul Mount

into the wrist area. It is associated with several incarnations, and in its true form, is a rarity to find. The accompanying print (figure 58) belongs to an attractive forty-five-year-old female journalist and mother of two who has survived many trials and tribulations in her life. She is a skeptic when it comes to alternative belief practices, yet, doesn't shut the door to possibilities. Like many excellent reporters, she questions everything.

The mounts add an important dimension to the hand. They provide information that touches at the very core of the person's likes and dislikes, and uncover hidden attributes and strengths, which are important elements to a health profile.

XI

TELLTALE HAND MOVEMENTS AND POSITIONS

The movement and placement of our hands and fingers tells us how we are feeling inwardly about ourselves, or toward those with whom we come in contact. The movements portray feelings of power, weakness, threat from our surroundings, cultural adaptations, likes, and dislikes.

We can also discern the mood of others by taking note of their hand movements. When we're feeling down, troubled, or ill, we frequently clutch our thumb inside the fist, perhaps a small gesture of the return to the womb where it is safe and comfortable. Hand movements can also show our reaction to a given situation. For example, if we're uncomfortable in a group of people we may place our hands behind our backs, or grasp them together.

I can recall walking into several different gatherings where I felt uncomfortable. My hands seemed to be dragging on the ground, so I would seek more comfortable postures such as sticking a hand in a pocket, clutching my shoulder bag, or placing them in my lap when I was able to sit down.

Our hand movements, then, reflect our inward states and moods. When we're sick, our hands seem listless and tired. They reflect our brains at work, when we want to escape the chatter of others, or even the thoughts of our own minds when we're feeling down. But the brain keeps working, no matter how sluggish or active we become, and our hand movements show it.

If we want to, we can actually change movements we find undesirable. To do so, though, requires a reshuffling in our brains. Skilled orators know how to do this. They might be feeling sick or grumpy, but they don't let the audience perceive their true moods. As their words flow, and they alter hand movements to go with what they are saying, their moods might also change for the better.

Even if we're not public orators and we're feeling listless, we can sometimes change that feeling by maybe shouting "yahoo," making a fist, and throwing a power punch into the air.

It's similar to changing our handwriting for self-improvement. "Grapho-Therapeutics" holds that the character can be changed by repetitive handwriting exercises. "In effect, then, when we voluntarily undertake to change a sign in our handwriting through repetitive exercise, we are giving a powerful suggestion to the subconscious to effect the corresponding character change," Kathy Stevenson, a noted California graphologist, once told me.

As she further explained, handwriting is a neurological function in which the brain transmits signals down the nervous system to the muscles and the fingers, which push or pull accordingly, creating what we refer to as writing. Since scientists now know of the hand-brain connection, even its association to touch (see Chapter 1), it follows that changing our hand movements changes the mapping in the brain.

Some people are extremely sensitive to hand movements and positions. I observed two friends once, a man and woman, in heated political discussion. The man, trying to make a point, was jabbing his index finger toward the woman. She stopped the conversation saying, "I divorced a husband one time for continually pointing a finger at me like that."

Even our spiritual outlook is manifested in hand movement, either by training or a natural feeling that causes us to turn the palms outward when giving blessings toward the heavens, or palms down, when giving blessings toward the earth. Some religions, such as Christianity, call for palms up during worship, while the adherents of some older religions, who paid respect to earthly spirits in trees and rocks, turned palms down in worship.

Obsessive hand washing is seen as a mark of innocence, and/or a reaction to the culmination of childhood fears, genetics, and the environment, according to mental health experts. Several treatment strategies, including psychotherapy, biofeedback, meditation, and certain drugs are used to alleviate obsessive-compulsive disorders (OCD). Changes in diet, too, are sometimes used to treat OCD.

Ritual hand washing is sometimes used in religious ceremonies serving as a symbol of purity. It is also used as a symbol to alleviate guilt, as in the case of Pontius Pilate who washed his hands from the responsibility of the death of Christ.

THE CURL

When the hand is in a relaxed position, observe the "curl" of the fingers. The more the *curl*, the less secure the person feels. If the fingers are held *straight*, it indicates self-confidence. If particular fingers are curled, rather than all of them, it indicates a specific difficulty concerned with the meaning of that finger. It can be a temporary condition and when the problem is resolved, the finger will return to its normal position. When specific fingers are curled, the shape of the finger indicates certain character traits:

○ When only the ring finger (Apollo) and the little finger (Mercury) bend downward into the palm in a curl, it signifies someone who's afraid to speak out at the moment. The subject may be one of sensitivity, or the person may not yet be familiar with the subject. This finger posture can sometimes be an unwillingness to face the truth.

○ Often, curling of the fingers is temporary and when the problem is solved and the person feels more comfortable, the fingers take on a straighter appearance.

○ If the ring finger is the only one curled and the rest, including Mercury, appear straight, the person is deliberately withholding information. Often these people have glib tongues and appear to be great communicators.

○ If the little finger seems to stand out on its own, away from the other slightly curled fingers, the person tends to be individualistic.

Several chronic diseases manifest themselves in hand tremors. Hyperthyroidism is a gland disorder that accelerates body processes. It is characterized by slightly shaking hands that shake more when the fingers are spread apart. Parkinson's disease, caused by damage to brain cells, has many symptoms, one of which is a pill-rolling movement of the fingers, as if the person has a small pebble or pill between the thumb and other fingers and manipulates it around and around.

SPACING

Another example of how the hands reflect our mental state is to place the palms down on top of a table. Note whether the hand is placed flat on the table or if it is arched. The higher the arch, the less sure the person is feeling of him- or herself. If the palm is flat on the table, the person feels in control of the situation.

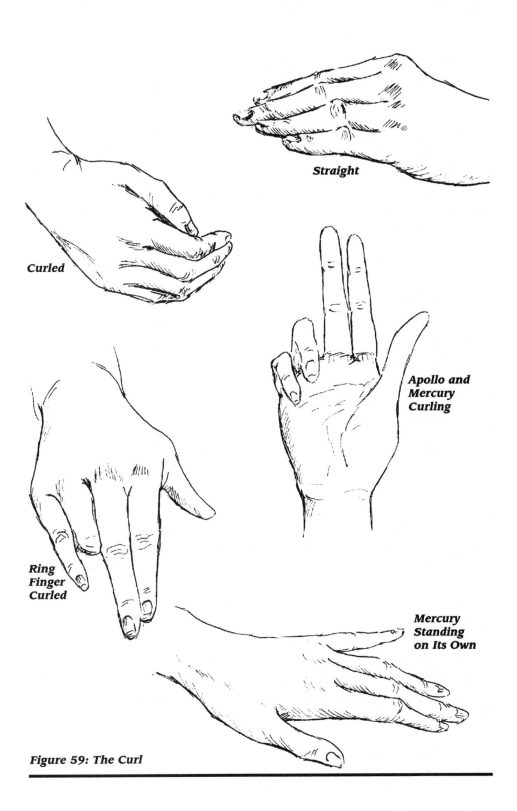

Straight

Curled

Apollo and Mercury Curling

Ring Finger Curled

Mercury Standing on Its Own

Figure 59: The Curl

Also note the distance between the two hands when a person has both hands on the table. If the hands are spaced wider apart than the breadth of the shoulders, the person is ready for business, maybe even a little aggressive. The problem is, though, in this position, the person is long on ideas, and short on following through with them.

If the space is equal to the shoulders, a balance between producing ideas and completing projects is established. The spacing of the hands and certain fingers indicate many things about a person:

○ When the hands are close together, the person is being cautious about any planned changes. He or she wants to stick to the familiar.

○ Note if the hands are generally spread open or clenched. If the fingers have spaces between them when the hand is in a relaxed position, the person is open-minded. When cramped together, even in a relaxed position, the person is narrow-minded.

○ Tact, diplomacy, and perfectionism can be shown when the thumbs are touching.

○ Hands touching when laid out flat indicate inhibition and conservatism.

○ Hands open and hanging limply at the side of the body indicate indecision.

○ Constant change of hand positions shows confusion.

○ Arms folded across the chest with the hands tucked inward indicates someone who has doubts about what is being said by another person.

MORE HAND SIGNS

Though the years, the meanings of particular hand movements have accumulated in American culture. Here is a list of some of the many gestures you can watch for, which can provide several types of information about an individual:

○ A clenched fist can be both good and bad. A gently clenched fist is a sign of needed determination, and a

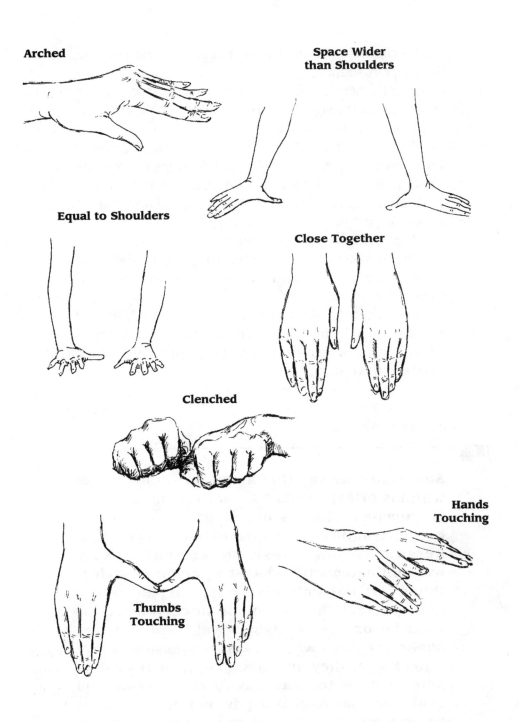

Arched

**Space Wider
than Shoulders**

Equal to Shoulders

Close Together

Clenched

**Hands
Touching**

**Thumbs
Touching**

Figure 60: The Spacing

tightly clenched fist may show unrealistic determination, anger, or frustration.

○ A tightly clenched fist with the thumb tucked beneath the fingers is the sign of a miser not only with money, but with his or her approach to life.

○ When the thumb is tucked into a loose fist, the person has a guilt complex or is trying to hide some event in his or her past. It can also indicate extreme anxiety.

○ When the thumb looks tense, stiff, or tied down to the hand, the person is feeling intimidated.

○ Hands clasped together with the fingers entwined is a sign of someone contemplating his or her next move, especially when the fingers are held beneath the chin.

○ When the hands are placed together without the fingers entwining, but with the thumbs wrapped around each other, the person is waiting for another person's next move.

Sometimes we say that a certain person "talks with his or her hands." Actually, someone who is animated with his or her hands is showing an alert nature—one interested in the other person. When these movements seem uncoordinated with what the person is saying, though, it not only distracts, but makes the listener feel the person is uncertain about what he or she is saying. We've all watched public speakers whose hand expressions don't reflect what they are saying. President Bush is notorious for this, as was former presidential contender, Michael Dukakis. Former President Reagan was a master of hand use. So was Sir Winston Churchill.

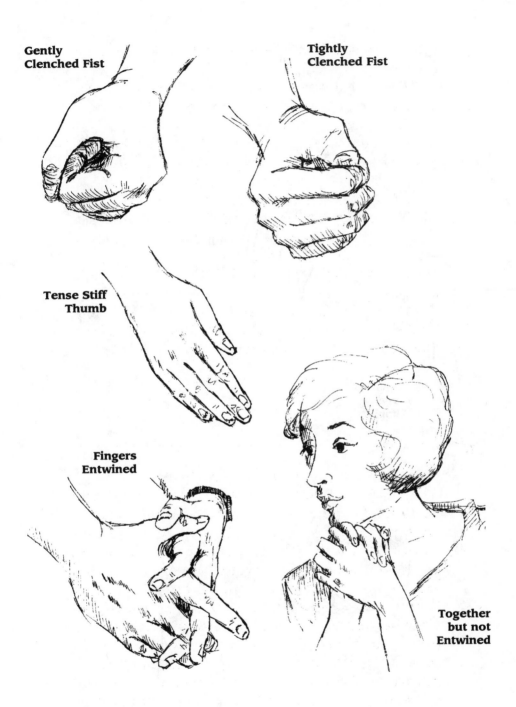

Gently Clenched Fist

Tightly Clenched Fist

Tense Stiff Thumb

Fingers Entwined

Together but not Entwined

Figure 61: More Hand Signs

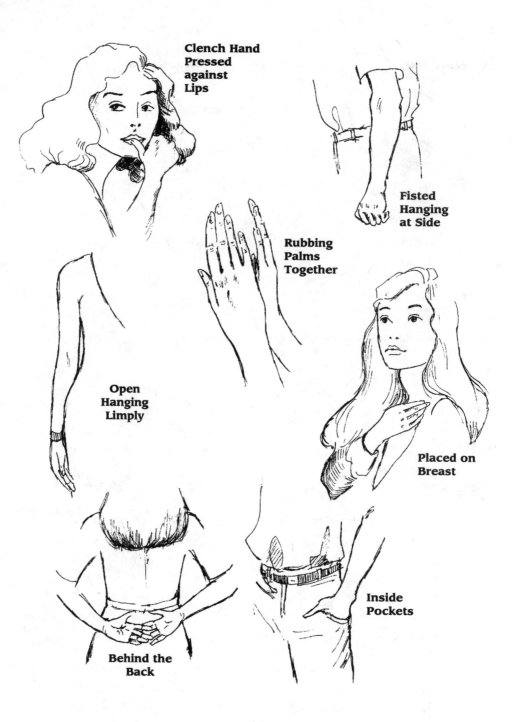

Clench Hand Pressed against Lips

Fisted Hanging at Side

Rubbing Palms Together

Open Hanging Limply

Placed on Breast

Behind the Back

Inside Pockets

Figure 62: More Hand Signs

○ If the hand is clenched and the thumb is pressed against the lips, the person is contemplating his or her own next move.

○ Rubbing the palms together can indicate a cunning nature.

○ Fisted hands hanging by the side indicate strong will and determination.

○ Open hands hanging limply by the side show indecision.

○ The hand placed on the breast signifies an attitude of knowledge.

○ Hands placed behind the back indicate people who are attempting to size up a situation. They may be temporarily unsure of themselves.

○ When people hold their hands inside pockets, they may be trying to conceal something, or at the least, show caution in revelations.

Observing a person's hand movements need not be restricted to palm reading. Much can be learned about politicians, religious leaders, and speakers of every persuasion simply by watching their hands. It sometimes provides information not available just by listening to them.

Observing the hands in magazine and newspaper photos can also provide insight into a person's character. Former President Richard Nixon was frequently pictured with his hands clasped together, fingers entwined. Former President Ronald Reagan, during a press conference, was captured on film with his Finger of Apollo bent toward the palm, an indicator of withholding information. Former President Jimmy Carter was shown several times in photos with his hands in a fist hanging by his side, an indication of strong will and determination.

XII

HEALING HANDS

Exploring the dimensions of touch not only enhances one's well-being, but puts one in touch with one's own caring and natures. Hands can energize, relax, and heal both the person touching and the person being touched. It becomes an exchange of energy that places individuals in the center of the universe, where time and space are integrated into healing power.

TOUCH FOR HEALING

Today, as in times of old, the healing touch, or laying on of hands, is recognized by some in the established medical profession.

This healing touch has been recognized in all societies, from ancient Greeks to Native Americans. It is mentioned in the Old and New Testaments; kings of Western culture have been accorded the healing touch, and Eastern traditions from time immemorial practiced it.

The touch of the fingers and the laying on of hands had been, since its earliest history, a gesture of blessing and healing. Tribute was paid to certain Greek gods and goddesses for their power to heal. And before them, and still today, many primitive tribes ascribe their chiefs and medicine men with the healing touch.

Paul Tabori writes in *The Book of the Hand* that the kings of England and France were believed to possess the power to cure with healing hands. "Some historians believe that the faith in the royal

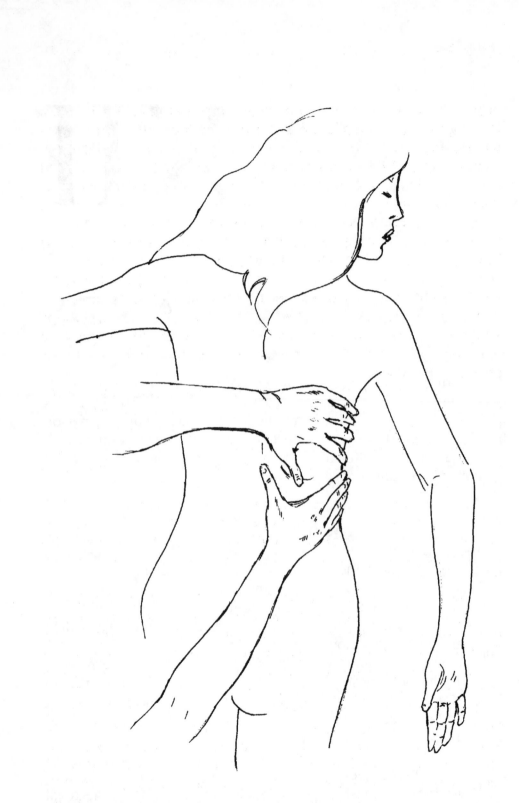

Figure 63: Massage can revitalize the body and spirit

healing hand spread from the Romans to the Germanic tribes. But it is unlikely that they needed to borrow such a belief; the Anglo-Saxon kings traced their descent directly to Oden or Woden, the supreme god of the North, a father of spells, and a magician and healer. The hand wielding the sacrificial knife was, at the same time, the healer's hand."

Unfortunately, Western medicine, especially that practiced in the United States, long ago discarded the idea of touch being part of healing, even when combined with modern technology. Fortunately, in some medical circles, it is was reintroduced, but not until the 1920s when practitioners demonstrated that neglected infants, mostly in orphanages, simply died from the lack of being touched. By the end of World War II serious studies on the effects of touching for all ages were underway, and many physicians recognized its significance to the health of individuals.

Millions of tiny receptors concentrated more abundantly in the skin of the hands and fingertips than any other place on the body, so the hands are highly attuned to heat, cold, vibrations, strength, weakness, and changes in these sensations. In combination with a sensitive and caring individual, is it any wonder that some possess the healing touch?

Yet, it is also unfortunate that the idea of healing through touch draws upon some of the worst elements in American society, sometimes reaching lunatic proportions. I remember one TV evangelist who promised cures for watchers who would place their hands on top of their television sets.

Syng Kyu Yu, a California practitioner who practices Lama-style finger pressure, once told me that a true finger pressure artist must also have love and compassion for his patients. Whether it's acupressure, Shiatsu, Do-In, reflexology, a baby massage, hands-on healing, or just plain hugging, people can benefit by rediscovering the benefits of stimulating the physical senses by touch.

In the 1992 spring issue of *The Magazine*, a publication of Rush Presbyterian-St. Luke's Medical Center, Chicago, Judy Friedrichs, M.S., R.N., recounts that when therapeutic touch is used in a soothing environment, tiny and premature babies have stronger heart rates, more even respiratory rates, and eat better. Linda Hollinger, Ph.D., R.N., says that the elderly in nursing homes also thrive with touch, and have less depression.

Many other methods, in addition to just plain touching and hugging, have proven to be beneficial. Some are listed because I have experienced them as a reporter, have some felt knowledge, and found them effective. Yet, I wouldn't discard traditional medicine with its modern technology that has helped to provide the Western world with a life span unheard of one hundred years ago. It is well to remember, too, that improved diets have helped with this increase. Despite these advances, though, as part of the human condition, we still get sick. The care and bonding that accompany the healing touch can enhance traditional forms of medicine, and surely, mainstream practitioners can learn something from this "hands-on" approach. Actually, as individuals, most of us can benefit by touching others and being touched.

I say "most" because time, place, and individual likes and dislikes must be taken into consideration for touching to be effective. I recall once covering a week-long metaphysical convention when "hug therapy" was coming into vogue. Because I was there as a reporter, one member of the hug therapy group kept jumping out at me with a big hug every chance he got in an effort to draw attention to his group.

Since I was milling about trying to pick up good stories for the newspaper on a variety of subjects, it became quite annoying. Also, some people, for whatever personal or physical reason, don't like being touched.

Sesame and olive oils are often used by a masseur (man), or masseuse (woman), to assist the hands in moving smoothly over the body. The oil can be scented with such essences as lemon, orange, marigold, cinnamon, clove, vanilla, almond, coconut, anise, red raspberry, and mint. Chamomile and cloves serve as skin softeners, while lemon and marigold are useful as cleaners. It is best to use the oils at room temperature, and for the one giving the massage to warm the oil in his or her hands before applying, rather than pouring the lotion on the person's body.

THERAPEUTIC TOUCH PRACTICES

Many newer hands-on, touch techniques, several that combine age-old methods with modern physiological knowledge, and, in some cases, psychotherapy, are being used in growing numbers to combat stress, to revitalize the body, and to heal.

Some touch practices, such as acupuncture, chiropractic, and osteopathy require state licensing, and carry strict codes of conduct. Others, such as the massage therapies, and some hands-on-techniques combined with psychotherapy, require no special, or additional licensing in most states, so it serves the client well to ask about the person's training and background, or to check them out through other sources such as accrediting associations affiliated with their discipline (see list on pages 185-86).

Although some therapists, such as osteopaths and acupuncturists, are schooled to give medical diagnosis, many other types of practitioners are not.

Osteopathy

Osteopathy involves touch, and is practiced by specially trained doctors with a sub-specialty in manipulation of joints, muscles, and tissues as an option to some medications and traditional treatment. Osteopaths are required to have four years of college based on premedical requirements, and then attend four years at one of the osteopathic medical schools throughout the country. Many osteopaths deal in "family medicine," and say the term "holistic" medicine is not new to them, and was built into their practices more than 110 years ago. Osteopathic physicians often correct structural problems by manipulating the position of bones in order to treat a wide range of health problems. Again, this speciality utilizes the sense of touch to facilitate healing.

Chiropractic

Chiropractic is ranked as the third largest health care profession in the Western world with nearly $2.5 billion spent annually on spinal manipulation, mostly in the treatment of back pain. Chiropractic is not accepted by many in the established medical profession, but in the past ten years has gained wide acceptance in some areas, especially in sports medicine. It wasn't until 1984 that the Olympic Organizing Committee officially recognized chiropractic, and for the first time allowed chiropractors to work with American athletes in the Olympic villages. Prior to that time, they set up camp on the outskirts of the villages since security passes were needed for entrance. The athletes, themselves, demanded it.

Although chiropractic, as we know it today, can be traced to the late 1800s, spinal manipulation was known, and practiced, in the time of Picrates. Modern chiropractic is generally attributed to have begun at the turn of the century, and now boasts about forty thousand practitioners in the United States. It is recognized as a legitimate form of medical treatment by most medical insurance companies.

Although some chiropractors claim to cure many ailments through spinal manipulation, traditional medicine is skeptical about these claims, and believes chiropractic should contain itself to skeletal manipulations. One thing not disputed is that chiropractic flourishes because of the "hands-on" techniques used by practitioners, which is often missing in mainstream medicine. The touch of another human being seems to hold healing properties regardless of the name by which it goes.

Reflexology

Reflexology is a technique that claims to stimulate nerve endings and energy meridians through a reflex point in the feet or hands that stimulates a corresponding organ or gland. One can apply reflexology to themselves, but the hands-on approach by a trained practitioner can be a soothing experience, similar to one of the many types of massages. Once when writing an article on reflexology as a reporter, a local reflexologist, Edward Kaufman, gave me a treatment, and I was energized for the rest of the day. To this day, I can still visualize his hands. They were huge, and looked clumsy, but I called them "magic hands" in the article. Never have I felt such energy coming from someone's hands.

Kaufman recommends clients see a physician if he believes the person suffers a chronic condition, or might have a debilitating disease. Too, we can practice a bit of reflexology on ourselves. By massaging the lower part of the big toe at the crease closest to the foot, and just above it, we can relieve tension. I've massaged this spot deeply to relieve headaches. Running the fingers between the toes also relaxes a person. Grabbing the ends of each toe between our fingers and twisting them acts as a stimulant.

Acupressure

Based on traditional Chinese healing, acupressure is a type of bodywork healing that uses specific body points to stimulate the flow of energy or "chi" in the body, and to clear obstacles in the body's total energy flow. This flow, or force, is called "prana" in Yogic terms. It is used to bring the body and mind into harmony. Practitioners and adherents believe this vital energy flows throughout the body along meridians in specific directions, and that by connecting the energy flow of the twelve major organ meridians, balance can be restored. Traditionally, 365 acupoints exist, and finger pressure at these points helps restore the balance of energy.

For example, to relieve headaches, press your thumbs on the eyebrow ridge in the dip about midpoint. This is where the supraorbital nerve approaches the surface. Press hard using circular motions. Many other forms of acupressure exist, such as finger-pressure, Shiatsu, and the Do-In, which is self-acupressure, utilizing some of the acupressure points.

Shiatsu

A form of Japanese finger pressure, shiatsu is a therapeutic massage practiced in China and Japan for centuries. It is based on theories underlying most oriental medicine, and incorporates the fourteen major meridians that run through the body serving as conduits of dynamic energy.

These meridians are located in the arms, legs, and trunk and control the vital forces of the major organs of the body. The practitioner primarily uses his or her thumbs and palms on the pressure points, sometimes gently, sometimes with great pressure. Some practitioners use their knees or feet. Some are gentle, and some cause discomfort, believing that it gets to the problem more quickly.

Particular points on the meridians, called tsubo, absorb and discharge energy. Practitioners believe that when these points are hard, dull, or painful, the corresponding organ is affected. The practitioner then uses his or her hands to stimulate, strengthen, or energize the problem organs. The practitioner uses pressure to calm overactive organs, while using his or her own energy to achieve this balance. I once experienced a shiatsu massage while doing an article on a mineral springs spa in Brea, California, and found it very invigorating. The photographer who accompanied me also had one, plus a hot body wrap. He fell asleep and I waited for hours not knowing what had happened to him.

Myotherapy

Myotherapy, one of the newer forms of touch for healing, involves strong pressure on areas called "trigger points," throughout the body. These trigger points are similar to those used by physicians who treat muscle pain by injecting anesthetics into specific areas of muscles that serve as trigger points of pain. It was developed in the mid-1970s by Bonnie Prudden while working with a physician who was using anesthetics in the trigger points to ease the pain. She discovered that applying heavy pressure to these trigger points could achieve the same results as injections. She continued working with physicians to further develop the method, and the school that teaches the method bears her name.

Rolfing

Rolfing is an intense form of massage, is used for emotional release, and involves deep tissue manipulation to realign the muscles. Widely used by some psychotherapists, it was developed by Ida Rolf, Ph.D. Central to rolfing is manipulating connective tissues back into their proper places to allow gravity to contribute energy to the body. It can be a painful process. It was to me, and I left the session feeling sore. But a few days later my muscles felt rejuvenated and better than ever. Rolfers undergo extensive training, and are certified by the Rolf Institute.

Feldenkrais

Through Feldenkrais, participants learn to use their bodies more effectively through breathing, body movement, and brain exercises. It also employs touch massage to guide the body in more effective movements. It was developed by Moshe Feldenkrais, an engineer and physicist with degrees in mechanical and electrical engineering.

The touching involves bends, rolls, turns, twists, and pushes on the body to make it more aware of the process by which it moves. Awareness Through Movement (ATM) involves simple exercises designed to get the brain and body coordinated. Certified practitioners usually complete a four-year training course.

Some palm readers believe that cosmic or universal energy enters the body through the fingers of Jupiter (index) and Mercury (little finger). When excess waste or unused energy leaves the body, the fingers of Saturn (middle finger) and Apollo (ring finger) act as the conduit. Some, too, believe that when we hold the hands of other people, we are picking up those people's energy fields.

Polarity Therapy

Polarity therapy involves bodywork, diet, exercise, and self-awareness. The practitioner uses his or her hands to assist the flow of healing energy in the client's body, and teaches a type of Yoga designed to create relaxation and balance through self-help energy techniques. An all-encompassing technique, it promotes the use of specific dietary principles for internal cleansing and long-term maintenance, an understanding of the sources of a person's tension, and ways to overcome tension in order to sustain health. Polarity therapy was developed by the late Randolph Stone, a chiropractor, who believed and taught that body, emotions, mind, and spirit are interdependent.

Palpation

Tradition physicians, too, use touch in examining patients. Palpation is used to feel the texture, size, feel, and location of parts of the body. Palpatory percussion, whereby physicians use light pressure with the flat of the hand, is used by doctors to examine body movement.

Massage

Many forms of massage exist, but anyone who has undergone such treatment usually feels lighter, energized, and calmed. The most common, "Swedish Massage," designed to improve muscle tone, employs long smooth strokes toward the direction of the heart. Trigger-point massage goes more deeply into the muscles causing them to relax.

Yet, anyone can learn to massage, and no name or label is needed. Many good books on massage are available, and the practice is quite easy. Often, the one giving the massage feels invigorated by touching another person and making him or her feel good.

Touch Healing or Laying on of Hands

Touch for healing involves energy transmission from one human being to another. Some practitioners believe that the energy they pass on to others derives from a universal field of energy that unites all living and nonliving matter together as a whole. Some "psychic" healers claim they use their own body energy to balance out their clients' body energy in order to eliminate physical or emotional disturbances. It is claimed that healers have an excess of life energy which they can bestow on other people.

Ethical practitioners don't give medical diagnosis unless they suggest a visit to the doctor; don't predict death or disease; don't give advice; or make a client dependent upon future visits, with the stipulation of more money. Some people, more than others, seem to possess "the healing touch."

Many nurses have long known the power of hands-on healing. One of them, a registered nurse working at a southern California hospital that I once interviewed, is called upon by physicians to use her abilities on weaker newborn babies in the unit where she works. The energy from her hands seems to give the weaker babies additional strength immediately.

During another interview, a man talked about going to a psychic healer for help with aorta stenosis (improperly functioning heart valves). He said, "She placed her hot little paws on me and got me to the point where the pain was gone," he said.

This same healer demonstrated her technique by having me lie upon a table while she slowly guided her hands about five inches from the front side of my body. Before long I could feel the heat from her hands on the area of my solar plexus near the stomach. Those who scoff at such ideas may say that it was mind over matter, and perhaps it was, but at the time, I was playing the typical cynical reporter, although I tend to be open to new experiences. Paula B. Slater and Barbara Sinor, author of *Beyond Words*, call touch healing, "love current," adding that "it is out of our love nature that touch brings healing."

Numerous studies have shown that infants neglected of human touch suffer emotional and developmental problems, and stunted growth. In extreme cases, they sometimes wither and die. This need to touch and be touched stays with us most of our lives, and has been with us since the dawn of humans.

Several different types of therapy and healing practices involving touch have been mentioned in this chapter. Yet, one needn't wait until one needs therapy or healing to use the magic of touch. Simply practicing the joy of touch in everyday activities enhances life and invigorates the soul. It secures our place as full members of the human community residing on planet earth.

Information about any of the practices listed in the chapter can be obtained by contacting the following agencies:

Osteopathy: **American Osteopathy Association, 142 E. Ontario St., Chicago, IL 60611, (312) 280-5800.**

Chiropractic: **1701 Clarendon Blvd., Arlington, VA 22209, (202) 276-8800.**

Reflexology: **Associated Bodywork and Massage Professionals, 1746 Cole Blvd., Ste. 225, Golden, CO 80401, (303) 674-8478.**

Acupressure or *Shiatsu*: **American Association of Acupuncture and Oriental Medicine, 4101 Lakebone Trail, #201, Riley, North Carolina 27607, (919) 787-5181; American Oriental Bodywork Association, 50 Maple Place, Manhasset, NY 11030; Jin Shin Do Foundation for Bodymind (Oriental Healing), 366 California Ave., Ste. 16, Palo Alto, CA 94306, (415) 328-1881; American Association of Oriental Healing Arts, P.O.B. 718, Jamaica Plain, MA 02130, (617) 522-0251.**

☞*Myotherapy*: The Bonnie Prudden School for Physical Fitness and Myotherapy, Box 59, Stockbridge, MA 01262, (413) 298-3066.

☞*Rolfing*: Rolf Institute, P.O.B. 1868, Boulder, CO 80306, (303) 449-5903.

☞*Feldenkrais*: Feldenkrais Guild, 14550 W. 99th, Lexexa, KS 66215, (913) 492-1444.

☞*Massage*: American Massage Therapy Association, 1130 W. N. Shore Ave., Chicago, IL 60626-4670, (312) 761-AMTA.

☞*Polarity Therapy*: American Polarity Therapy Association, P.O.B. 1517, E. Arlington, MA 02174, (617) 641-2200.

☞*Infant Massage*: Association for Infant Massage, c/o Leslie Day (director), 79th St., Boat Basin, Box 9, New York, NY 10024, (212) 877-1268.

Glossary

ACUPRESSURE: Chinese bodywork healing using specific pressure points to stimulate and balance the flow of the body's energy.

ACROMEGALIA: Medical condition with body parts growing inordinately large.

AFFECTION LINES: Small horizontal lines running beneath the little finger above the Line of Heart on the percussion side of the hand (sometimes called "marriage lines").

AIR HAND: Astrological name referring to elongated and often pointed shape.

ALLERGY LINE: Horizontal line running along the base of the Mount of Luna near the wrist bracelets.

ANTIBODY OR MARS LINE: Attendant line running inside the top of the Line of Life.

APOLLO: Roman sun god. Name of a mount, the ring finger, and a line running vertically through the palm toward finger so named.

ARCH: Ability of fingers or thumb to curve backward from the palm.

ARTHRITIS: Medical condition of many forms, predominantly osteoarthritis and rheumatoid arthritis, causing pain and swelling.

ATTENDANT LINE: Also called "sister" or "backup" line, that runs parallel to another line and adds strength.

AUTOIMMUNE SYSTEM: A bodily system of defense against infection.

AUTONOMIC NERVOUS SYSTEM: Part of the nervous system regulating vital bodily function not under conscious control.

AXONS: Nerve fibers.

BACKUP LINES: Smaller lines running parallel and adding strength to major and minor lines.

BEAU LINES: Horizontal ridges across fingernails.

BRACELETS: Also called "rascettes," or "wrist bracelets," found just beneath palm on wrist.

BRACHIAL: Main artery of the upper arm.

BREAK: Refers to breaks in lines.

CAPILLARY LINES: Faint lines drooping from major or minor lines that sap energy.

CARPAL TUNNEL SYNDROME: Medical condition with damage to the middle nerve and tendons of the hand.

CEPHALIC LINE: Small line running next to Line of Health.

CHAIN: Chain-like grouping on some lines.

CHILDREN LINES: Short vertical lines running upwards from the affection or marriage lines.

CHIROPRACTIC: Treatment of disease originally based on manipulation of body joints and spine to restore normal nerve function.

CHROMOSOMES: Threadlike structures in the center of a cell that carry genetic information.

CIRCLE: Small marking usually found on lines, in a group or on mounts.

CLUBBED FINGERS: Tips of fingers shaped like clubs and indicating various diseases.

CLUBBED THUMB: A bulbous shaped tip.

COLLAGEN: A protein that forms connective tissue.

CONCAVE NAILS: Refers to depressed area in center of nail.

CONGENITAL: Conditions present at birth.

CONIC: Tapered, pointed fingers or tapered, full hand.

CONIC FINGERTIPS: Fingertips with a slender, tapered shape.

CONVEX NAILS: Nails that curve over the fingertip.

CORE: Approximate center of skin ridge print.

CROSS: Found independently in palm, on lines of hand, or when major lines cross.

CROSS BARS: Group of independent crossed lines.

CURIOSITY LINE: Short horizontal line on the Mount of Jupiter near the side of the hand.

CURLING: When a finger or fingers bend inward.

DERMAL RIDGES: Raised patterned lines in certain spots on the palm and on the fingertips.

DERMATOGLYPHICS: Scientific study of skin-ridge patterns.

DERMATOLOGIST: Physician specializing in skin care.

DEVELOPED MOUNTS: Puffy areas of the palm generally beneath the fingers, the thumb, and on the percussion side of the hand.

DIABETES: Medical condition of several forms affecting sugar use by the body.

DISTAL: Part of the hands farthest from the wrist.

DISTAL TRANSVERSE CREASE: Horizontal line known in classical palmistry as the Line of Heart.

DOMINANT HAND: Right or left hand preferred use.

DOTS: Tiny, solid circles found on the palm and some lines.

DOWN'S SYNDROME: Birth defect resulting in mental retardation of different degrees, accompanied by physical defects.

DUPUYTREN'S CONTRACTURE: Medical condition with thickening and tightening of tissue beneath the skin of the palm.

DYSLEXIA: Blockage of reading ability stemming from a variety of disorders.

EARTH HAND: Astrological name referring to square- and solid-shaped hand.

EARTH MOUNT: Health indicator as shown by the puff on the back of the hand when the thumb is pressed against the side of the pointing finger.

ECTOMORPH: Fragile, slender body shape.

ELASTIC SKIN: Generally refers to firm, yet pliable skin, or mounts.

ELASTIN: Protein that forms a type of elastic tissue fiber.

ENDOMORPH: Large trunk and thighs, with soft, round body shape.

EPIDERMIS: Outer layers of the skin.

ESCAPE OR AVOIDANCE LINE: Horizontal line appearing at the bottom of the Line of Life.

FELDENKRAIS: Exercise and treatment utilizing the body more effectively through breathing, body movement, and brain exercises.

FILBERT NAILS: Wide at the base and round at the tip.

FINGERS OF: Apollo, ring finger; Jupiter, index finger; Mercury, little finger; Saturn, middle finger.

FINGERPRINTS: Dermal ridges on the tips of the fingers.

FINGER SHAPES: Conic, square, and spatulate tipped.

FIRE HAND: Astrological name referring to a hand that is wider at the bottom or the top and tapering to the opposite end of the palm.

FIRM-JOINTED: Minimal backward bend or arch.

FLEXIBLE FINGERS: Fingers that arch back toward back of hand.

FLUTED NAILS: Vertical grooves on the fingernails.

FORKS: Branches at beginnings or endings of lines, usually adding strength to the line.

FRATERNAL TWINS: Two offspring developed from two eggs fertilized at the same time.

FRIENDSHIP LINES: Horizontal lines on the Mount of Venus not touching the Line of Life.

GENETIC: Transmission of characteristics from one generation to another.

GESTATION: Period of fertilization of egg to birth.

GIRDLE OF VENUS: Horizontal lines running above the Line of Life.

GRILLES: Cross-hatched lines usually meaning misfortune.

HANDEDNESS: Propensity toward use of either right or left hand.

HAND SHAKE: Grasping another's hand and usually pumping it up and down.

HEALER'S MARKS: Short vertical lines on the Mount of Mercury.

HIPPOCRATIC NAILS: Also called "watch glass" curve over the fingertip and resembles the face of a watch.

HYPOTHENAR: Scientific term for the Mount of Luna on the percussion side of the hand.

IDENTICAL TWINS: Developed from a single fertilized ovum.

INDULGENCE LINE: A small slanting located on the wrist at the bottom of the Mount of Luna indicating a propensity to self-indulge.

INTERDIGITAL: Skin areas between fingers.

ISLANDS: Small, oval-shaped markings indicating weakness on the lines in which they appear.

JUPITER: Chief Roman god or deity. Name of index finger, and mount beneath it.

KERATIN: A protein found in skin, hair, nails, and tooth enamel.

KERATOLYSIS: Abnormal shedding of skin.

KNOTS: Bulge in joints of fingers.

KNUCKLES: Referred to as third joints nearest the palm.

LADDERS: Small bunches of lines crossing main lines.

LEFT HAND: Usually the nondominant hand.

LINE OF APOLLO: A line on the palm running toward the Mount of Apollo.

LINE OF FATE: Palm line referring to work, careers, and ambitions.

LINE OF HEAD: Major palm line referring to intellect.

LINE OF HEALTH: (Hepatica), running vertical from the direction of the little finger toward the palm.

LINE OF HEART: Major palm line referring to love and friendship capabilities.

LINE OF LIFE: Major palm line referring to quality of life potential.

LINE OF STUBBORNNESS: Located on thumb near bottom of second joint.

LOWER MARS MOUNT: Located inside the Line of Life within the arch made by the thumb.

LUNA: (Latin name reference) Associated with Selene, a moon goddess, and Artemis or Diana. Mount on lower portion of palm on the percussion side of the hand.

LUNULA: Half-moon at the base of the fingernail.

MAJOR LINES: Lines of Life, Head, and Heart in classical palmistry, and called palmar or flexion creases by scientists.

MARS: Roman war god. Palm contains upper and lower mounts of Mars.

MARFAN'S SYNDROME: Inherited medical condition related to excess bone length.

MASSAGE: Several forms of body work involving touch.

MATRIX: Base of the fingernail.

MELANIN: Naturally occurring dark color in the skin, hair, and parts of eyes triggered by melanocyte cells in the body.

MERCURY: Roman messenger of the gods. Refers to the little finger, and the mount beneath that finger.

MESOMORPH: Body shape with prominent muscles and bones with long arms and legs.

MOON LINE: Sometimes called the "Line of Intuition," a small line curving into the palm and resting between the Mounts of Luna and Mercury.

MOUNTS: Raised portions on the palm beneath the fingers, surrounding the thumb, and encompassing portions of the palm on the percussion side of the hand.

MOUNT OF APOLLO: Found beneath the ring finger on the palm.

MOUNT OF JUPITER: Found beneath the index finger on the palm.

MOUNT OF LUNA: Found on the percussion side of the hand below the Line of Heart and running toward the wrist.

MOUNT OF MERCURY: Found beneath the little finger on the palm.

MOUNT OF NEPTUNE: Located just above the wrist bracelets on the palm between Venus and Luna.

MOUNT OF PLUTO: Located on the lower part of the palm near the wrist bracelets on the percussion side of the hand.

MOUNT OF SATURN: Found beneath the middle finger on the palm.

MOUNT OF VENUS: Found surrounding the thumb and inside the Line of Life.

MYOTHERAPY: A form of touch therapy involving pressure on certain trigger points on the body.

MYSTIC CROSS: A well-formed cross made by two independent lines crossing one another and located beneath the Mount of Saturn between the lines of Head and Heart.

NEURONAL: Having to do with the nerve cells in the central nervous system.

OLD SOUL MOUNT: Large area encompassing the Mount of Pluto on the percussion side of the hand near the wrist bracelets.

OSTEOPATHY: Medical treatment involving manipulation of joints, muscles, and tissues as opposed to medications and traditional medical practice methods.

PALMAR APONEUROSIS: Connective tissue surrounding muscles of the palm.

PALMARIS LONGUS: Long, slender muscle of the forearm.

PALMAR METACARPAL ARTERY: Artery that supplies blood to the fingers.

PALM-CHIN REFLEX: A medical condition caused by nerve abnormalities.

PALPATION: Medical examination by touch.

PARASYMPATHETIC NERVOUS SYSTEM: Part of the autonomic nervous system.

PEPTIC ULCER: Related to a breakdown of mucous membrane in the digestive system.

PERCUSSION: The little finger side of the hand running to the wrist.

PETROGLYPHS: Carvings in rock.

PHALANGE: Three sections of the fingers between the joints.

PHILOSOPHIC HAND: Referring to long, tapering full shape.

PICTOGRAPH: Painted picture using symbols.

POINTED FINGERS: Sometimes referred to as conic.

POLARITY THERAPY: Therapy involving bodywork, diet, exercise, and self-awareness.

PROXIMAL: The part of the hand closest to the wrist.

PROXIMAL TRANSVERSE CREASE: Horizontal line known in classical palmistry as the Line of Head.

PSORIASIS: Inborn skin disorder.

PSYCHIC HAND: Referring to long, flat, and slender shape.

QUADRANTS: Four sections or categories of the palm.

RADIAL: Referring to thumb side of hand.

RADIAL ARTERY: A branch of the main artery of the upper arm.

REFLEXOLOGY: Stimulation of nerve endings and energy meridians through reflex points in the feet or hands.

RIGHT HAND: Usually the dominant hand and the one read for the present and future.

RING OF SATURN: Small line found beneath the Saturn finger.

RING OF SOLOMON: Small line beneath the finger of Jupiter, sometimes referred to as the "Ring of Jupiter."

ROLFING: An intense form of massage involving deep tissue manipulation.

SATURN: Roman god of agriculture. Denotes middle finger and mount beneath that finger.

SCHIZOPHRENIA: A group of mental disorders resulting in the loss of reality.

SHIATSU: Therapeutic massage using finger pressure incorporating the body's major meridians.

SHORT NAILS: More broad than long.

SICKLE CELL ANEMIA: An incurable blood disorder.

SIMIAN LINE: Lines of Head and Heart combined and running horizontally across the palm.

SKIN RIDGE PATTERNS: Encompassing fingerprints and found on palm mounts and skin between the fingers.

SKIN TEXTURE: Thickness of skin involving depth and breadth of skin ridges.

SMOOTH FINGERS: Without protruding joints.

SPATULATE HAND: Shaped wider at the bottom or the top and tapering to the opposite end of the palm.

SPATULATE TIPPED FINGERS: Flattened, broad fingertips, shaped like a spatula.

SPOON NAILS: Having concave area in middle of the nail.

SPOTS: Tiny dots found on lines or mounts.

SQUARES: Small markings usually surrounding a break in a line, island, circle, spot, or latter.

SQUARE HANDS: A palm nearly equal in breadth and length.

SQUARE-TIPPED FINGERS: Blunted, with little roundness at tip.

ST. ANDRES'S CROSS: Lateral line near the wrist between the lines of Health and Fate.

STIFF FINGERS OR THUMB: Unable to arch toward back of hand.

SYMPATHETIC NERVOUS SYSTEM: Part of the autonomic nervous system.

SYMPHALANGIA: An inherited condition marked by stiff fingers and toes joined in a webbed effect.

TACTFUL PADS: Pads on the inside tips of the fingers.

TASSELED LINE: Lines that end or begin with tassles.

TEMPER LINE: Found directly above the second joint on the thumb.

TERATOGENS: A substance or process that blocks normal fetal development.

TESTOSTERONE: Hormone that stimulates growth of male characteristics.

THENAR EMINENCE: Scientific term for Mount of Venus, the mount beneath the thumb.

THUMB BUMP: Also known as "philosopher's bump," and found on the lowest joint of the thumb.

TOUCH HEALING: Sometimes called "laying on of hands," involves energy transmission from one human to another.

TRIRADIUS, TRIADII (plural): Center point of three projections of curved patterns in a dermal ridge print.

ULNAR: Scientific term for the percussion side of the hand.

ULNAR ARTERY: A branch of the main artery of the upper arm.

ULTRAVIOLET RAYS: Light beyond range of human vision, damaging to skin.

UPPER MARS MOUNT: A mount on the percussion side of the hand beneath the Line of Heart and near the Mount of Luna.

VOLAR PADS: Same as dermal ridge as in fingerprints.

VENUS: Also known as Aphrodite, Roman or Greek goddess of love and beauty. Major mount on the thumb side of the hand.

VIRTUAL FINGERS: Cerebral instructions to the hands.

WATER HAND: Astrological name referring to tapering, well-padded hand shape and tapering fingers.

WRIST BRACELETS: Lines cutting across wrist just below the palm.

ZYGODACTYLY: Finger and feet webbing.

Bibliography

"Ame... urnal of Physical Anthropology." Vol. 72, No. 2, February 1987.

Briggs, ... e in the Crucible. Los Angeles: Jeremy P. Tarcher, Inc., 1990.

"Bulletin ... sychonomic Society." Vol. 25, No. 2, p. 82-84. 1987.

Cummins, ... d. *Fingerprints, Palms and Soles: an Introduction to Dermatogly...* arold Cummins and Charles Midlo. Philadelphia: Blakiston Co., 1943.

Holt, Sarah B. ... *Genetics of Dermal Ridges* with an introduction by L.S. Penrose. Spring... linois: Thomas, 1968.

"Journal of Abnor... ychology." Vol. 96, No. 2, p. 89-93. 1987.

Lee, Linda and Jam... arlton. *The Hand Book*. Englewood Cliffs, New Jersey: Prentice-Hall, Inc., 1...

Loesch, Danuta Z. Q... *ative Dermatoglyphics: Classification, Genetics and Pathology*. Oxford, New... : Oxford University Press, 1983.

Restak, Richard, M.D. *The...* n. New York: Bantam Books, 1984.

Slater, Paula B., and Bar... Sinor. *Beyond Words*. Middletown, California: Harbin Springs Publishing, 1...

Tabori, Paul, *The Book of ...Hand*. Philadelphia and New York: Chilton Company, Book Division, 1962...

Wolff, Dr. Charlotte. *A Psycholog...f Gesture*. New York: Arno Press, A New York Times Company, 1972.

Murphy, Michael, *The Future of ... Body*. Los Angeles: Jeremy P. Tarcher, Inc., 1992.